I'm Not Being Fed

Discovering the Food that Satisfies the Soul

I'm Not Being Fed

Discovering the Food that Satisfies the Soul

JEFF CAVINS

West Chester, Pennsylvania

Ascension Press
Post Office Box 1990
West Chester, PA 19380
Orders: 1-800-376-0520
www.AscensionPress.com

Cover design by Kinsey Caruth

Printed in the United States of America
07 08 09 10 11 6 5 4 3 2

ISBN 978-1-932645-33-0

Dedication

To Bishop Paul V. Dudley, Retired Bishop of Sioux Falls, South Dakota, whose teaching and example created in me a deeper hunger for the Eucharist.

Contents

Key to Biblical Abbreviations

The following abbreviations are used for the various Scriptural verses cited throughout the book. (*Note*: CCC = *Catechism of the Catholic Church*.)

Old Testament

Gn	Genesis
Ex	Exodus
Lv	Leviticus
Nm	Numbers
Dt	Deuteronomy
Jos	Joshua
Jgs	Judges
Ru	Ruth
1 Sam	1 Samuel
2 Sam	2 Samuel
1 Kgs	1 Kings
2 Kgs	2 Kings
1 Chr	1 Chronicles
2 Chr	2 Chronicles
Ezr	Ezra
Neh	Nehemiah
Tb	Tobit
Jdt	Judith
Est	Esther
1 Mc	1 Maccabees
2 Mc	2 Maccabees
Jb	Job
Ps	Psalms
Prv	Proverbs
Eccl	Ecclesiastes
Sng	Song of Songs
Wis	Wisdom
Sir	Sirach
Is	Isaiah
Jer	Jeremiah
Lam	Lamentations
Bar	Baruch
Ez	Ezekiel
Dn	Daniel
Hos	Hosea
Jl	Joel
Am	Amos
Ob	Obadiah
Jon	Jonah
Mi	Micah
Na	Nahum
Hb	Habakkuk
Zep	Zephaniah
Hg	Haggai
Zec	Zechariah
Mal	Malachi

New Testament

Mt	Matthew
Mk	Mark
Lk	Luke
Jn	John
Acts	Acts
Rom	Romans
1 Cor	1 Corinthians
2 Cor	2 Corinthians
Gal	Galatians
Eph	Ephesians
Phil	Philippians
Col	Colossians
1 Thess	1 Thessalonians
2 Thess	2 Thessalonians
1 Tm	1 Timothy
2 Tm	2 Timothy
Ti	Titus
Phlm	Philemon
Heb	Hebrews
Jas	James
1 Pt	1 Peter
2 Pt	2 Peter
1 Jn	1 John
2 Jn	2 John
3 Jn	3 John
Jude	Jude
Rv	Revelation

Introduction

The #1 Catholic Eating Disorder

"I wasn't being fed!"

It happened again; someone recognized me at a social event and approached me with an explanation as to why she had left the Catholic Church. "I heard that you went back to the Catholic Church," she said. "That's wonderful for you. I was in the Church for thirty years, but I had to leave because I wasn't being fed."

I knew what she was trying to say because I, too, had once been there. I had turned away from the Catholic Church with the same words, "I wasn't being fed." In my early twenties I put everything Catholic behind me and embarked upon a journey into the world of Protestantism. The woman's comments made me think of the many times I've heard people say similar things: "I'm not getting what I need in the Catholic Church," "I just need more of the Word of God," or "The Church isn't meeting me where I'm at right now. I need to be fed somewhere else." I pictured a myriad of faces of people who had left the Church to attend an evangelical church, or to join an independent charismatic fellowship, or to take interest in an Eastern religion. You may have thought the same thing on occasion: "I'm not being fed."

Wanting to be fed is perfectly normal. Hunger is actually a good thing, as it alerts us to our real need. All of us need to be fed, physically and spiritually. We need food. We need spiritual sustenance.

This need to be fed is a biblical theme that runs from Genesis to Revelation. On the physical level, there is the dramatic story of the Hebrews fleeing Egypt and then crying out for food in the desert, murmuring against Moses and Aaron: "And the sons of Israel said to them, 'Would that we had died by the hand of the LORD in the land of Egypt, when we sat by the fleshpots and ate bread to the full; for you have brought us out into this wilderness to kill this whole assembly with hunger'" (Ex 16:3). God responded by sending down *manna*—the miraculous bread from heaven. And after being fed in that way for a while, what did the people do? They grumbled and complained. They thought back to how good they had it as slaves in Egypt, eating fish, cucumbers, melons, leeks, onions, and garlic (see Num 11:5). I can just hear them saying, "I'm not being fed the way I like. I want more. I want better!"

As the saying goes, the grass is always greener on the other side, but is this so? How often do we think that we'll be satisfied with a different car, a new house, a better job, or a fitter body? How often do we convince ourselves that the music will be better at *that* church, the sermons more exciting when preached by *that* pastor, or our spiritual hunger will be satisfied by *that* group, church, movement, book, tape, prophet, leader, speaker, or televangelist? How often has God provided sustenance for us and we have responded by complaining? How often has God provided a miracle for us and we have responded by whining? "I'm not being fed here, God, can't you see? Why can't you feed me what I want to eat?"

The first few chapters of the Bible provide a striking example of how dangerous it can be to satisfy our hunger by doing things our way. Adam and Eve had everything that anyone could ever want: a comfortable life free from manual labor, nice weather, perfect pets, and communion with God—in short, Paradise. And yet, tempted by Satan in the Garden, they went looking for food in the wrong place and for the wrong reasons.

The serpent succeeded in tempting the father and mother of mankind. The key to his strategy was to promise Eve that, by eating of the tree of the knowledge of good and evil, she would have a better life, she would know more, and she would be "like God, knowing good and evil" (Gn 3:5). It really didn't seem to be that big of a deal. Seeing that the tree was good for food, and that it was pleasant to look at, she ate from the tree, and then "gave also to her husband with her, and he ate" (Gn 3:6). Adam and Eve had the perfect life and the perfect cuisine—and it still wasn't enough.

The point here is not that a Catholic who leaves the Church after thirty years is a bad person. The reference to Adam and Eve simply highlights the fact that all of us are hungry and need to be fed; all of us are tempted to satisfy our hunger in ways that *seem* good and pleasing, but are not truly good for us, nor are they God's will. We are all tempted, like Jacob's brother, Esau, to sell our birthright for a bowl of porridge. It might be great porridge and it might satisfy us for a while, but it's not enough; it's not what God desires for us.

My birthright, as a baptized Catholic, was the grace of the sacraments, especially the grace of the Holy Eucharist. Not that I deserved it—no one does. But by God's grace I was born into a Catholic family and had access to the family meal, the sacrifice of Jesus Christ, presented under the appearance of bread and wine. And yet I walked away. I rebelled against my earthly father and my heavenly Father. I looked at the Eucharist—the most miraculous of meals and perfect of sacrifices—and turned away. Obviously I didn't understand the meal that had been set before me. I thought I would be better fed elsewhere.

Like the Hebrews wandering in the desert, I had to learn a painful lesson in humility. "And he humbled you and let you be hungry," Moses tells the people in the book of Deuteronomy, "and fed you with manna which you did not know, nor did your fathers know, that he might make you understand that man does not live by bread alone, but man lives by everything that proceeds out of the mouth of the Lord" (Dt 8:3). I spent twelve years as a Protestant pastor thinking that I didn't need the Eucharist and that I could live by the Bible alone. Ignoring the full revelation of God, I missed the beautiful truth about Jesus offering His Body, Blood, Soul, and Divinity. For twelve years I was in the desert crying out, "I wasn't being fed!"

This book is a response to all those who have walked away from the Catholic Church because they believed they weren't being fed. It is meant to be an encouragement to those Catholics who sometimes question why they remain in the Church. It is also my own mini-*Confessions*, the story of how I walked away from the Bread of Life and then came back as a prodigal son, welcomed with open arms by my heavenly Father and His family, the one, holy, catholic, and apostolic Church. It is a reflection on the sublime, awesome mystery of the Eucharist, the "source and summit of the Christian life" (CCC 1324) and "the sum and summary of our faith" (CCC 1327). And it is a commentary on chapter 6 of John's Gospel and Jesus' Bread of Life discourse, one of the most powerful passages of the New Testament.

King Solomon wrote in the Proverbs, "The Lord will not allow the righteous to hunger" (Prv 10:3). My prayer is that the Lord will open our hearts even more to the truth of His love, and that He will show us how, because of that great love, He offers us the perfect meal of the Body and Blood of the One who makes us righteous by His death and resurrection.

My purpose in writing about this topic is not to be combative, negative, or militant. I simply need to tell it like it is, and to proclaim the awesome food we have as Catholics. Do you have a spiritual eating disorder? Don't lose heart! Jesus said, "I am the bread of life; he who comes to me shall not hunger, and he who believes in me shall never thirst" (Jn 6:35). The table is set, the meal is prepared, and the Lamb is waiting.

Chapter 1

I Left the King's Table

I was raised in the Catholic Church of the 1960s and early 1970s, a time when people believed in the "eighth sacrament" of Holy Osmosis: you drop your kids off at church and they miraculously learn everything they need to know about the Faith. It truly would have been a miracle if it had worked. It *didn't* work for me, though, nor did it work for most Catholics of my generation. Faithful Catholic parents made sure their children attended Mass each week, sent them to Catholic school, or enrolled them in a religious education program, and saw to it that they received the sacraments. The problem was that my generation was caught up in a rapidly-changing Church, one trying to get its bearings after the Second Vatican Council. The purpose of Vatican II was to help the Church become more effective in proclaiming the Gospel to the modern world. Though the primary intent of the council was to clarify and refocus the role of the laity, religious life, and the liturgy, in the confusion that followed, the Church's perennial teachings were often not adequately or faithfully communicated in all their fullness.

A Normal American Catholic Boy

My story is typical of the post-Vatican II generation. I grew up in a loving, caring family, and we attended Sunday

Mass every week and observed holy days of obligation at our suburban parish church. All I remember about my CCD classes was a pretty blonde girl. While I enjoyed the atmosphere of church, I could not explain what was happening during the different parts of the Mass. Though I sensed the importance of my responsibility to the Church on the day of my Confirmation, I didn't receive any further instruction on what to do with this commitment. I received from my parents a St. Joseph Edition of the Bible, and I treated it with awe and reverence. It sparked an interest and craving for Scripture in me that very day, but my sudden zeal gradually diminished as sports, parties, and girls filled my time.

Yet I continued to have a hunger for God. I was drawn to the idea of God and to that vague but attractive notion of "the Holy." During my sophomore and junior years of high school, I became obsessed with candles and books on spirituality, including many works on Eastern mysticism and meditation. With candles scattered throughout my room, I would read books such as *The Tibetan Book of the Dead* and *Zen and the Art of Motorcycle Maintenance.* I was trying hard to tune in. "God," I would pray, "If you are real, speak to me. I have to know that you are real!"

The problem was that, despite my sincere efforts and my constant reading, I never really knew who Jesus was. I knew almost nothing at all about the Catholic Church and what I, as a Catholic, should believe—not to mention *why* I should believe it. I didn't understand the sacraments, and I didn't know what the Eucharist was—or rather, *who* the Eucharist is. The Rosary was a mystery to me, as was the solitary candle lit by the tabernacle. Why did we cross ourselves with our thumb on the head, lips, and heart before the Gospel reading? I had no idea. Why did Jesus come and die on the Cross? I had no clue. Why should I be a Catholic and not a Hindu, or a Buddhist, or a Hare Krishna? I had no explanation.

By the time I headed off to college to study broadcasting, I was open to almost anything. Not long after the start of my first semester, I remember an evening when I was driving down the road, an eighteen-year-old college freshman, crying out to God—whoever He might be—"I don't care if you're Buddha, I'll serve you! If you're Confucius, I'll follow you! Just reveal yourself to me!"

I Finally Find Jesus

It was in my first year of college that I started to turn to Christ in a deliberate way. It began when I met a young lady named Emily in one of my classes. Not only was she beautiful; there was something different about her that I couldn't put my finger on, a confidence and calm that was visible. For nearly two weeks I was preoccupied with her, until I finally found the courage to ask her out. With some hesitancy she accepted my invitation to go bowling one evening.

Before we even got out of her driveway, she turned to me and asked, "Do you know Jesus Christ as your personal Savior?" Huh? What in the world was she talking about? I had never heard anybody talk that way about Jesus before. It intrigued me. "Well, yeah," I stammered, searching for an answer that would win her over, "I'm Catholic." I was not prepared at all for her next question. "Do you speak in tongues?" she asked. Never before in my life had I heard the phrase "speak in tongues." I hesitated, not wanting to give the wrong response. "As a matter of fact, I do," I lied, desperate not to lose her interest. This seemed to satisfy her, so I thought I would keep the ball rolling, even though I had no idea what she was referring to. I wanted to sound like I knew what I was talking about, so I thought I would ask her a similar question. The problem was that I couldn't remember whether she had said "speak in tongues" or "lips." Figuring that I had a fifty-fifty chance, I ventured to ask, "Do you speak in *lips*?" exposing my ignorance of Pentecostal terminology. She corrected me graciously and the conversation moved on.

Between gutter balls and greasy food, Emily told me all about her relationship with Jesus. I was fascinated. I had never heard someone speak about Jesus in such a personal way; she knew that Jesus was her friend, and she spoke about Him as naturally as she would about the weather. She told me about reading the Bible every day, learning more about Jesus' love for her. I wanted what she had. There I was—a comedian, class clown, and rock 'n' roll junkie—wanting to hear more about Jesus and the Bible. The hunger for God had never died; it had only been buried beneath bad jokes and wild '70s clothing.

I began meeting with Emily and her mother for daily Bible study in their home. I was fascinated by her mother's well-worn Scofield Reference Bible. It was filled with commentary and notes about the passages we studied, and we would talk about how to apply what we read to our lives. I couldn't believe how much I enjoyed it; I was finally learning about God and Jesus in a way that whetted my appetite for more. One night, on my way home from one of these visits, I pulled the car over to the side of the road. Filled with emotion, I began to weep. "Jesus!" I cried out, "Come into my heart." I wanted a new start, a new beginning. I was ready to give my life to Jesus.

Something happened at that moment that I didn't realize for many years. As I said "Yes!" to Jesus, I was really saying "Yes!" to my baptismal promises. When I had been baptized as a baby, my parents had promised to raise me in the Catholic Church and to teach me about Jesus. Baptism was just the beginning of the journey of salvation, but I had gotten derailed years earlier. At that moment, sitting alone in my car, I sensed I was really on track with God. Even though I would use terms such as "born again" and "saved"—phrases and words more common to Protestants than to Catholics—I was in communion with God and the Church. I knew at that moment, tears running down my face, that I would spend the rest of my life proclaiming Jesus and sharing the Gospel with anyone and everyone I could.

Cracks in My Catholic Life

I felt that I was finally being fed the spiritual food I had been craving. I had no intention of leaving the Catholic Church at that point; I just wanted more of Jesus. I was excited to tell my parents about my newfound relationship with the Lord. I drove home and quickly went inside. When my mother saw my red eyes, she exclaimed, "What happened to you?" She must have thought that Emily had just dumped me, or that I had been drinking.

"Mom, I've been born again!" I exclaimed, bursting with joy.

"What?" Her face went ashen.

"I got saved tonight!" I couldn't understand why she didn't share my excitement. Didn't she know how wonderful this news was? Couldn't she see how important this was to me?

"Don't you say that!" she said. "You were a Christian the day you were baptized."

And that was it—she didn't want to hear anything more about it. But I knew that something had happened. I was different, but my parents didn't understand the difference. It was the start of tension that would drive a wedge between my parents and me for years to come, causing division and pain for all of us.

I wanted to buy a Bible. I wanted to meet others who enjoyed discussing their faith. I wanted to go to confession. So I went to my parish to see the priest. When I found him, I immediately told him, "Father, I've been born again!" His reaction was similar to that of my mother. I pressed on. "Father, will you bless my new Bible? I just bought it." With a sober expression on his face, he mumbled something about "that's not what we do in the Catholic Church." But he relented and blessed my Bible. Then I asked to go to confession. After all, I wanted as much of Jesus as I could get.

I soon found a Catholic charismatic prayer group at my parish and started studying with them weekly. Their meetings were lively and inspirational; they were people who truly seemed to have a personal relationship with Jesus. In addition, Emily began to take me to various non-denominational churches, where the preaching was passionate and the worship exhilarating.

I couldn't stop reading the Bible; I was addicted to it. Some days I would read it from 9:00 at night until 4:00 in the morning. I carried it with me everywhere, and I would talk to anybody at any time and any place about Jesus.

I kept going to Mass with my parents, but I was also attending the local non-denominational church with Emily and her family. I started to notice the difference between Catholics and "Bible Christians." The Catholics I knew seemed to be stuck in a lifestyle that was boring, drab, and mandatory. There seemed to be no joy, no spark. But the Bible Christians were upbeat and friendly, and they couldn't stop sharing their love for Jesus. They had made a conscious decision to follow Jesus and be His disciple, but the Catholics didn't appear certain of what they believed or why they went to Mass. But I still didn't see a need to leave the Catholic Church.

That would begin to change when I decided to go to Bible college. I had come to the conclusion that I wanted to spend time studying Scripture under the direction of professors devoted to the lifelong study of God's written word. I wanted to be that sort of person, teaching others about the Bible and Jesus and sharing the Gospel. My parents were not thrilled with my new direction in life, resulting in a fight the night before I left home to attend Bible college in Texas. "Why are you doing this?" my father asked me angrily.

"I want to study the Bible," I told him, "and I want to give my entire life to Jesus."

"But you're a Catholic and you're going to a Protestant school!" he said, clearly upset. "And how are you going to provide for yourself?"

"Jesus will provide," I said, "Jesus will take care of me." At that moment, my father did something he had never done before in his life. He hit me, knocking me to the ground. As I stared up at him from the floor of my room in disbelief, I was filled with hurt and anger. "Why?" I yelled, "Why?" He didn't respond. "I am no son of yours!" I shouted. He turned and walked out of the room.

"I'm Outta Here"

Emily and I left for Texas the next day. We had become engaged shortly before, and a year later we were married at my home parish of St. Hubert's in Chanhassen, Minnesota.

As I was growing up I dreamed of being a broadcaster on television or radio. So after our wedding and the completion of Bible college, I attended broadcasting school in Minneapolis. Upon finishing school there, I wasn't sure what step to take next, so I took a job as a disc jockey at a rock 'n' roll station in North Dakota. It was there that I finally left the Catholic Church.

The final straw was when I attended a dance sponsored by my parish. Kids were dancing and listening to music filled with overt lyrics about sex, while the parish priest and the parents looked on. Nobody seemed bothered in the least. I was appalled and decided that I'd had enough—I was finally fed up with the Catholic Church. While my opinions about the Church were skewed by my strained relationship with my family, I came to view most Catholics as spiritually blind, lukewarm, and indifferent to the things of God. While these Catholics danced and partied and seemed unconcerned with sharing the Gospel, the people at the local Assembly of God congregation were going door-to-door sharing the good news of Jesus. Those were the *real* Christians, I thought, and they were the ones I wanted to be associated with.

A few days later, I heard that the bishop of the diocese was coming to the parish for a yearly open meeting. I decided that I would go and express my frustrations with the Church. Little did I know how expressive I would be! As I sat and waited for the meeting to begin, I suddenly became aware of how upset I was. I was literally shaking with anger, filled with rage at my father, the Catholic Church, and the local priest. I was angry that I had not "been fed" as a Catholic. I had not been taught about Jesus or the Bible or what I thought it meant to really be a Christian. I was full of hunger and anger, frustration and confusion.

When the bishop opened up the meeting for questions, I quickly raised my hand. "Sir," I said, "I am so frustrated. I gave my life to Christ on February 14, 1977. I love Jesus, but there's no place for me in the Catholic Church. I've had it!" I completely lost it, and screamed, "From this day forward I am not Catholic!" I turned and began walking out of the meeting. The bishop called after me, "I want to talk to you later." With a shake of my head I said, "I don't know," and left.

The next morning I went to the local convent where I often attended morning prayer. Apparently someone had told the bishop about my morning habit, for he was waiting there when I arrived. He beckoned me over. "Tell me your story," he said with genuine concern. So I told him about my love for Jesus and the Bible, my frustration with the Catholic Church, and of my anger towards my father. He listened very intently as I poured out my heart.

When I had finished, the bishop said, "I want to tell you three things. First, this journey that you are on is from God. Secondly, I am going to call you 'little Newman,' because you have the same spirit and love for Scripture as Cardinal Newman." I didn't know who he was talking about. Then he paused and looked me right in the eye. "Thirdly, Jeff, there will be a day when you will return to the Church, and when you do, you will teach your people." I looked right back and said, "I don't think so." Then I stood up and walked out. I was done with the Catholic Church; I was going somewhere else to be fed. With hardly a thought about leaving the sacraments and all things Catholic behind, I made my exit. I had the Bible and I had Jesus—that's all I needed, or so I thought.

Dietary Deficiencies

I went on to be ordained and serve as a Protestant pastor for twelve years. Those were good years, filled with wonderful friends and warm fellowship. I loved teaching from the Bible, opening up Scripture for my congregation, and guiding them into a deeper appreciation of God's word. The churches I pastored were always busy with classes, Bible studies, evangelistic outreach, and all sorts of programs for families, adults, and children. As a Protestant, I believed in *sola scriptura*—the belief that Scripture alone is a sufficient guide for the Christian life. In addition, I taught that communion was merely a symbol and the Holy Spirit would lead us into all truth if we would but listen.

Slowly I began to sense that something was missing. Around my ninth year as a pastor I started having some small hunger pangs. I had been feeding on Scripture and fellowship, but there was a longing for more—what could it be? What was missing?

Some of my symptoms started years earlier when I began studying the Jewish background to the Gospels and Jesus' life. As I delved into the Old Testament and Judaism, I began to see things I'd never noticed before. The more deeply I went into Scripture and its historical context, the more glimpses I had of the Catholic Church. And of Tradition. And of the Eucharist!

In Genesis 22, for example, God asks Abraham to sacrifice his only son and heir, Isaac. But after he took Isaac up to Mount Moriah and prepared the altar, Isaac inquired as to the lamb for the sacrifice. Abraham assured Isaac that God would provide the lamb. Just moments before Isaac was to be sacrificed, God stopped Abraham. A ram caught in the bushes was substituted—a sacrifice was provided, but the search for the lamb that God would provide had just begun. Throughout Scripture, many lambs are mentioned—and I was well aware that the ultimate lamb is Jesus. "Behold the Lamb of God!" declares John the Baptist (Jn 1:29, 36).

And what does Jesus say about eating the Lamb? "Truly, truly, I say to you, unless you eat the flesh of the Son of man and drink his blood, you have no life in you" (Jn 6:53). This is shocking stuff; I wasn't sure what to make of it. I was also realizing, reluctantly, that the Word of God had come down to us through history in not one, but two forms: oral and written tradition (see 2 Thess 2:15). I saw that this teaching about the Word of God was what the people of the Old

Testament believed and what both Jesus and Paul taught. And I was fully aware that I didn't believe it.

While studying Exodus 12, I noticed that the Jews, in celebrating the Passover, not only had to kill an unblemished lamb and sprinkle its blood on the doorposts and lintels, they had to *eat* the Lamb. "And they shall eat the flesh that same night, roasted with fire, and they shall eat it with unleavened bread and bitter herbs" (Ex 12:8). Without eating the Lamb, the Passover was incomplete. What could this mean? Since Christ is the fulfillment of the Old Covenant, how could we possibly eat the Paschal Lamb of the New Covenant?

Before I knew it, a series of events occurred that made it evident that these issues were not going to go away. The bishop of the Charismatic Episcopal Church invited me to visit and investigate becoming an Episcopal priest. While there, I picked up a copy of Thomas Howard's *Evangelical is Not Enough*. Howard was a former Evangelical who became an Anglican in his twenties, in large part because of his love of the liturgy. I read the book quickly, enjoying the fact that someone else also experienced a hunger for more. Then I read the last page. Howard spoke of leaving the Anglican Church and becoming Catholic! His journey into Catholicism piqued my curiosity. Could it be that he had asked the same questions as I had? Could he have found the answers I was looking for? I tracked down his number and called him. My curiosity turned to fear when I learned that he had, in fact, asked the exact same questions. And look where the answers had led him!

There's No Place Like Rome

At a Catholic bookstore I purchased the newly-published *Catechism of the Catholic Church* and a video of Pope John Paul II's 1993 visit to Denver for World Youth Day. In the video there was a clip of a young woman watching in rapt attention as the Pope went by. Her eyes filled with love, she mouthed the words "He's so cool." For some reason that broke me, and I began to cry. I said aloud, "He is the Vicar of Christ! He is my father in the faith and those people are my family in Christ and I've left it all." I realized that I had made a big mistake many years ago when I left the Catholic Church. Now I wanted to turn it around and come back home. I wanted to be fed in the way Jesus intended.

Wanting to know how to return to the Church, I searched for my childhood pastor, whom I hadn't seen for over twenty years and who had since become a bishop. I called the diocesan office in Sioux Falls, South Dakota, and asked for Bishop Paul Dudley, not expecting to get through. To my surprise, he took the call immediately. I told him about my spiritual journey and mentioned my recent studies, which had convinced me that the Eucharist was indeed the meal Christ had provided for His Church.

"You need to fly out and visit me so we can talk about it," the bishop said.

I agreed, and the next week I was on my way to Sioux Falls. When I stepped off the plane, Bishop Dudley was waiting to greet me. "Welcome home, Jeff," he said.

During my visit with the bishop, he encouraged me to go to Franciscan University of Steubenville, Ohio, and study Catholic theology. I liked the idea but knew there was a lot of work to be done. First, I had to return home and talk to the elders of my congregation, New Covenant Fellowship in Xenia, Ohio. I was not looking forward to it. Over half of the people there, including several of the elders, were former Catholics. The next Sunday, I announced my decision to the congregation—it was one of the hardest things I have ever done in my life. Some of the congregation understood, but many were upset. They couldn't believe I would leave the "true faith" and return to the Catholic Church.

After informing my congregation, I knew I had to talk to my parents. My talk with them would have to wait, since my wife and I were committed to taking a group to Israel on pilgrimage. My mother arrived the day before the trip to stay with our daughter. That evening, the phone rang. It was the hospital—my father had suffered a heart attack.

When I was finally able to reach him by phone, I asked, "How are you doing, Dad?" I needed to know how serious his heart attack had been and whether I should pull out of the trip to Israel.

"I'll be all right," he tried to assure me. "Jeff, do one thing." He paused, "Take care of your mother and your sisters." I knew at that moment that he was not all right and that I couldn't go to Israel. "Dad," I told him, "I'm coming home."

Upon my arrival back in the Twin Cities, I met with a counselor who helped me realize that my hurt and anger towards my father was one of the main reasons I had rebelled against the Church. I saw clearly that I had left my Catholic Faith for emotional—rather than doctrinal—reasons. I had reacted out of anger, spite, and frustration. Now, looking back, I can say that I've never met anyone who has left the Church for truly theological or doctrinal reasons—they leave because of hurt or misunderstandings, or because they are attracted by the zeal for God they see in many non-Catholics.

Sorry Is the Hardest Word

Determined to apologize to my father for the resentment toward him in my heart, I met with him shortly after his heart surgery. "I have something I need to talk to you about," I told him. All I could think about was him hitting me and walking out of my room those many years before.

"Dad," my voice shook. After what seemed like an eternity, I finally got the words out, "I've rebelled against you. I'm sorry. I want to come home. I want to come back to the Church. I am sorry."

He looked at me. "You don't know what this means to me, Jeff." He paused, "I have to get this off my chest because I've thought about this every day for years. You remember the night before you left home?"

I nodded, my heart pounding. "I'm sorry, Jeff," he said, "I don't know why I hit you. I'm sorry." Once again, I was crying, but not alone. As we embraced, the pain melted away and the years of anger and frustration disappeared. A normal American Catholic boy was returning to the King's table to eat once again with the family of God.

Chapter 2

Where's the (Biblical) Beef?

Though I eventually returned to the Church, many others who walk away from their childhood faith never return home. They end up going to many different places. Some stop going to church altogether and become agnostic, at least in practice. Others react more strongly, becoming secular humanists and embracing a life of materialism. Others dabble in Eastern religions and New Age practices or join non-Catholic churches. Others still call themselves Catholic but rarely attend Mass.

Endless Denominations

There are nearly three hundred million people in the United States, nearly 25 percent of whom are Catholic, at least in name. That's about seventy million Catholics. Just over half of the American population is Protestant, with about 13 percent having no particular religious affiliation at all. Today, fallen-away Catholics make up the second largest "denomination," so to speak, in the United States. And it's safe to say, based on the numbers, anecdotal evidence, and personal experience, that a large number of those former Catholics are now Protestants. They are members of Baptist denominations, the Assemblies of God, the Church of Christ, the Church of God, the Mormon church, community fellowships, charismatic groups, "home churches," and a host of "non-denominational" denominations, to use a phrase coined by Jesuit Father Mitch Pacwa, S.J.

In 1980 it was estimated that there were nearly 21,000 Christian denominations in the world, rooted in more than 150 "ecclesiastical traditions." The 2000 edition of the *World Christian Encyclopedia* stated that the number of denominations had increased to 33,820—and this figure doesn't include all the groups that insist on their "non-denominational" status. For example, within the Baptist tradition, founded in the 1600s by Anglican minister John Smyth, there are today more than a hundred different denominations and sub-denominations, the largest group being the Southern Baptist Convention with about sixteen million members. There are also Colored Primitive Baptists, the Free Will Baptist Church, the General Association of Regular Baptist Churches, the National Missionary Baptist Convention of America, Old Time Missionary Baptists, Strict Baptists, and United Free Will Baptists. It's not just confusing; it's sad to see Christians so divided.

When I was a boy in the early 1970s, the latest Christian craze was the Jesus Movement. It was a youth phenomenon with members who had been in or around the counter-cultural scene of the late 1960s; many of them had been into drugs and anti-establishment activities. They were called by names such as "Jesus Freaks" and "Jesus People." Their church services were made up of exuberant singing and fiery preaching of the Bible with emphasis on evangelization. They made a splash for a while, but eventually the movement slowed down and its numbers dwindled.

Recently, however, several major newspapers ran articles about a new and exciting phenomenon called the "un-church" movement. One article stated:

> Membership is surging at nondenominational churches that emphasize personal spirituality and unabashed worship over institutional tradition. Many, in fact, avoid the "C" word—church—preferring to identify themselves as fellowships or ministries. Because they have no denominational affiliation and often don't track membership, such churches are typically missed by religion demographers. But 2001 survey data collected by the Hartford Institute for Religion Research suggests that as many as 10 million Americans attend an estimated 35,000 independent and nondenominational churches—or roughly 13 percent of the total population of congregations. ["Nondenominational churches on the rise," Associated Press, December 26, 2003]

The names of these "churches" offer some clues as to their general approach to the Christian life: The Journey, Pathways, The Next Level, Connected Life Church, The Crossing, New Life Church, Pierced Chapel. There is much that is good and admirable about the intentions of these groups. In most cases, they want to help others, they love Jesus (insofar as they know Him), and they are looking for fellowship with like-minded people. But there is much that is near-sighted and problematic about these groups as well. For instance, there is a lopsided emphasis on the individual, a rejection of order and authority, and much talk of "freedom" and "expression." It sounds great, but it's not very original, as anyone who lived through the 1960s and '70s knows.

Though many of those in the "un-church" movement talk of connecting with the past and of knowing and appreciating Church history, it seems that this "connecting" usually assumes rather shallow forms: lots of candles, incense, Celtic crosses, and some neo-Gregorian chanting.

A member of one "un-church" group says he likes the "freedom to worship without any denominational trappings. 'There's no Baptist twist or Catholic twist or any twist,' he says. 'You take what's there and you don't add to it—you're just free with Jesus.'" This is simply another way of saying that, after centuries of failure and miscues, they have finally figured out what *real* Christianity is all about. They insist that they come with a clean slate, without any bias or agenda. But the issue isn't whether someone has a bias, but whether they have the fullness of truth. Has the Church founded by Jesus failed, or has it held fast against the gates of Hades (Mt 16:18)?

What's Behind the Epidemic of Fallen-Away Catholics

These are the sort of groups that are attracting Catholics who are bored, disgruntled, indifferent, or simply curious. Many of these Catholics are just like me when I was growing up: poorly catechized, confused, and lacking a thorough understanding of their Faith. Others are attracted to the friendliness and energy they find in other groups but don't experience at Mass in their parish. Though each may have a different reason for leaving the Catholic Church, there are some common factors to be found. Noted sociologist Dean R. Hoge has pinpointed these factors and has placed them into five basic categories:

Family Tension Dropouts: These are Catholics who grew up in difficult family situations. Once they are old enough, they leave home and the Church, and rarely look back for many years. They might associate the Catholic Faith with legalism and strictness, or fault the Church for somehow creating or contributing to an unbearable home life.

Weary Dropouts: "I'm bored!" is the motto of these Catholics. They're tired of their experiences with the Church; they want something exciting and engaging. Perhaps they've been attending Mass out of a sense of obligation to parents, spouse, or children. As soon as they see their chance, they take off.

Lifestyle Dropouts: These dropouts ask themselves, *Why should I stay Catholic when my lifestyle is at odds with what the Church teaches?* Perhaps they are cohabitating, sexually active outside of marriage, living a homosexual lifestyle, or are divorced and remarried without seeking an annulment. In short, the Catholic Faith cramps their style—their lifestyle—and they'd rather not change.

Anti-Change Dropouts: These include Catholics who are frustrated—even angry—about the changes made in the Church by the Second Vatican Council. These people believe that Vatican II is responsible for the abuses and silliness they have endured. It also includes people who want to see *more* change, either back to pre-Vatican II customs or in a more "progressive" direction. They have grown tired of waiting for the Church to change to suit them. So they go elsewhere or nowhere at all.

Spiritual Need Dropouts: This is the group that I belonged to and the one that is focused on in this book. These are the people who say, "I'm not being fed! I need more!" They don't think their spiritual needs are being met in the Catholic Church, and so they start to look around at other options. They usually want more upbeat and informal worship, impromptu prayer, small Bible study groups, and a vibrant sense of community and fellowship. They want to be around people who love Jesus and aren't afraid to say so. They aren't satisfied with going to church once a week, but want to meet with other Christians several times a week, even on a daily basis, if possible. They are on fire for Jesus and frustrated by what they perceive to be roadblocks to expressing their passion.

I'm sure that you know someone—a friend, family member, or co-worker—who fits into one of these categories. Since the number of former Catholics makes up the second-largest religious "denomination" in the United States (trailing only those Catholics who have remained in the Church), you probably know more than one such person. People who are frustrated, angry, or indifferent. They are bored, irritated, or searching. They might explain that the Catholic Church isn't feeding them the spiritual food they need. They need better sermons, more exciting services, and more contemporary music. They want practical teaching.

Clueless About the Eucharist?

I eventually came back to the Catholic Church because of its beliefs and teachings, all of them thoroughly based in Scripture. But more than anything else, it was the Eucharist that brought me back to the Church. In retrospect, if I had understood the Eucharist when I was younger, I would never have left. Yes, I would have been frustrated at times, but I could have endured the frustration had I known then what I know now.

One problem is that so many Catholics simply have not learned their Faith. A few years ago it was widely reported in the Catholic press that nearly 70 percent of Catholics either do not believe, understand, or know that, by the action of the priest during Mass, Jesus becomes truly and fully present in the Eucharist. There are many reasons for this deplorable fact, including poor catechesis and too much focus on subjective feelings over objective truth. Pope John Paul II, in his encyclical *Ecclesia de Eucharistia* ("On the Eucharist and its Relationship to the Church," April 17, 2003), points out several other reasons:

> At times one encounters an extremely reductive understanding of the Eucharistic mystery. Stripped of its sacrificial meaning, it is celebrated as if it were simply a fraternal banquet. Furthermore, the necessity of the ministerial priesthood, grounded in apostolic succession, is at times obscured and the sacramental nature of the Eucharist is reduced to its mere effectiveness as a form of proclamation. This has led here and there to ecumenical initiatives which, albeit well-intentioned, indulge in Eucharistic practices contrary to the discipline by which the Church expresses her faith. How can we not express profound grief at all this? The Eucharist is too great a gift to tolerate ambiguity and depreciation (no. 10).

As John Paul II indicates, there is a failure at times among Catholics to understand and explain why non-Catholics cannot receive the Eucharist. So many times I've heard Catholics lament how "arrogant" and "insensitive" it is that their Methodist friend or Lutheran cousin is not allowed to receive Holy Communion. And it's not uncommon to hear of priests officiating at weddings or funerals and inviting everyone—Catholics and non-Catholics alike—to come forward to receive the Eucharist. Perhaps this is due to a fear of appearing judgmental or inhospitable at such important moments, but I think that it results chiefly from a failure to appreciate the Church's teaching and thinking about the Eucharist. If Holy Communion really is that—holy and communion—then those who are not in full communion with the Catholic Church, if allowed to receive the Eucharist, are unwittingly speaking a lie with their actions. They are saying that they are in full communion with the One, Holy, Apostolic, and Catholic Church, even though they are not. Protestant Christians might love Jesus Christ with their whole heart, soul, and mind, but it is still wrong for them to receive Him in the Eucharist.

We need to remember that our separated brothers and sisters in Christ are *separated* from us, even though this separation may not be due to a conscious decision on their part. The Church's teaching on this point doesn't mean that Catholics are better than Protestants or that Protestants cannot be holy and very godly people. On the contrary! There are many Protestants who appear to be living far holier lives than quite a few Catholics. We Catholics too often see receiving the Eucharist as a right, instead of a glorious and undeserved gift which is ours by God's grace alone. And so we as Catholics need to be in a state of grace before approaching the altar; we must examine our consciences and, if we have committed serious sin, refrain from receiving Holy Communion until we have confessed our sins and they have been forgiven in the sacrament of Reconciliation (see 1 Cor 11:27ff).

In short, Catholics always need to be deepening and growing in their knowledge and love of the Eucharist. As Pope John Paul II tells us, "The Eucharist, as Christ's saving presence in the community of the faithful and its spiritual food, is *the most precious possession which the Church can have* in her journey through history" (par. 9; emphasis added). Do we really believe this? Do we live this way? The Eucharist, as Vatican II teaches, is "the source and summit of the Christian life" (*Lumen Gentium*, 11). This means that "the other sacraments, and indeed all ecclesiastical ministries and works of the apostolate, are bound up with the Eucharist and are oriented toward it. For in the blessed Eucharist is contained the whole spiritual good of the Church, namely Christ himself, our Pasch" (CCC 1324).

This is why I wanted to write this book and share what's on my heart. I've traveled around the country and given many talks, hosted the program *Life on the Rock* on the Eternal Word Television Network (EWTN), and have spoken to people every weekday on radio, and one comment that I often hear is this: "Well, Jeff, good for you that you went back to the Catholic Church. I'm glad it works for you." The implication seems to be that I am some sort of junkie who kicked the Catholic habit for twelve years but finally gave in to temptation and lost my struggle. That's undoubtedly how some of my former Protestant friends see it, since they continue to pray daily for my soul and for my return to the "true faith." But the fact remains: It was my dependency on Jesus Christ, who is the Way, the Truth, and the Life, that led me back to the Catholic Church. It was my need for true food and drink—the flesh and blood of my Savior (Jn 6:55)—that brought me home to His Church. Now I want to proclaim this truth always and everywhere and to help others see what they are missing, ignoring, or misunderstanding about the Eucharist.

Blasphemy and Ignorance

There are two basic reasons why people say that they aren't being fed in Catholic Church: ignorance or blasphemy. Either they truly don't know what happens at Mass (i.e., they are ignorant) or they knowingly utter words of "hatred, reproach, or defiance" (CCC 2148) against the Eucharist (i.e., they are guilty of blasphemy). As the *Catechism* states, "the prohibition of blasphemy extends to language against Christ's Church, the saints, and sacred things" (CCC 2148). There are some who leave the Church because they have chosen to hate God and reject Him. We can see this sort of hatred in secular humanists who were raised Catholic but now reject Christianity and despise God. Some even make their hatred known publicly and become avowed atheists.

I am convinced, though, that most Catholics who say they "aren't being fed" and who walk away from the Church do so out of ignorance. They simply don't realize what they are doing or understand why they are doing it. There are different types of ignorance and many reasons why that ignorance exists, including lack of knowledge, indifference, slothfulness, ingratitude, lukewarmness, the cares of this world, the scandal caused by sinful Catholics, and even irresponsibility (see CCC 29, 2094). Let's take a look at some of these reasons and influences.

It's hardly a secret that, in general, Catholic catechesis and religious education has been inadequate for several decades. If Catholic children are taught that the Eucharist is only a nice symbol, a family meal, or ordinary bread and wine meant to help us think about Jesus, they aren't going to appreciate the truth about the Eucharist. It's hard to believe something if it's misrepresented or not presented to you at all.

This is especially true if they are being told that "all of us are Eucharist," as though there is no significant difference between Jesus' unique gift of Himself and the spiritual sacrifices that we offer up to God (1 Pt 2:5). A general lack of respect and reverence, whether at Mass or before the Blessed Sacrament, sends the message that there isn't anything special about the Eucharist. The same message eventually comes through, albeit more subtly, in the blurring of the distinction between the ordained priesthood and the "common priesthood of the faithful" (CCC 1591) that all Catholics possess by virtue of their baptism.

In common usage, indifferentism is a lazy attitude towards something. In a theological context, it is the attitude that there's no real difference between various religions or belief systems, that they are all pretty much the same. In this case, it would be the idea that a Protestant form of communion is just as good and substantial as the Catholic Mass—that any differences are minor and inconsequential. Such a slothful attitude toward the Eucharist demonstrates a spiritual laziness and immaturity. The slothful person won't acknowledge the gifts that God has given and won't return the love He has offered.

Lukewarm Catholics are those who hesitate to give God the love and worship that is due Him. To them God says, "I know your deeds, that you are neither cold nor hot; I would that you were cold or hot. So because you are lukewarm, and neither hot nor cold, I will spit you out of my mouth" (Rv 3:15-6).

There are other Catholics who are so caught up in worldly cares and activities that they don't take time to come to Mass, or to contemplate what the Mass is, or to spend time in prayer and study. They put in their obligatory 45 minutes every Sunday and leave right after receiving the Eucharist.

Others walk away from the Lord's Table and His Church because of stumbling blocks. Perhaps they leave because of the recent sex scandals, or because a parish priest or staff member has offended them. Then there are the Catholics who are simply irresponsible and careless about their Faith, ultimately because they did not guard what had been entrusted to them (see 1 Tm 6:20).

Many Catholics who leave the Church to join Fundamentalist and Evangelical groups aren't stridently opposed to Catholicism—at first. But they eventually become antagonistic toward the Church to some degree, since most of those groups have serious disputes with Catholicism. Many believe that Catholics are not saved (or that only a few are saved), and that it is God's will for all Catholics to leave the Church once they "accept Jesus" as their "personal Lord and Savior." As I pointed out earlier, it took me many years to break away completely from the Church of my youth. Later, as a Protestant pastor, I often contrasted what I perceived as the dead religion of Catholicism with what I considered a more vibrant Christian faith. In retrospect, I see that my judgments were based on what I observed in the outward lives of some Catholics rather than on the actual content of Catholic teaching.

Who's Cooking Your Spiritual Meals?

This raises two vital questions: *Who* has the responsibility to feed you, and *what* is he feeding you?

These are questions that all we need to ask ourselves, but this is especially so for non-Catholic Christians. Let's examine the first question, looking in particular at Fundamentalists and Evangelicals, whose ranks include many former Catholics. If that's who you are, let me ask you: who has the responsibility to feed you? Who is preaching the Word of God in your church? Who do you turn to for answers, counseling, and advice? Most likely that person is your pastor, and he (or she) is probably a good person who loves Jesus and is doing his (or her) best to feed you. He probably has three or four years of Bible college training, and your congregation looks to him each week to open up the Bible and feed you from it. This usually takes place in the form of a twenty- or thirty-minute sermon. But where does your pastor get his authority to teach? Are his views based on his own interpretation of the Bible, on his experience and education, or upon 2,000 years of Christian tradition?

What exactly is it that your pastor feeds you? He has probably said, "I have the responsibility to feed you, and I have to answer to God for how well I feed you." So he provides a lengthy sermon. He teaches doctrine, faith, and morals. The service has little liturgy or ritual; it is structured around the sermon. As a former Protestant pastor, I know that I was always judged most heavily on my sermon. Was the congregation inspired by it? Was I able to give them something to chew on and take home? Of course, there were other ways of feeding the congregation, including weekday

Bible studies, Sunday school, worship music, and special events and talks.

All of us, whether we are Catholic, Protestant, or otherwise, have a built-in hunger for God. But if we stop short of what God wants for us, the hunger pangs will remain. Each of us has a hunger in our heart, and we are searching for something to satisfy it. It's like having a late night craving for food, without being exactly sure what kind of food you want. You get up, open the refrigerator, and gaze at every shelf. Then you shut it and sit back down. Five minutes later you get up, go over to the cupboard, and look for something else. We are indeed restless until our hearts rest in God.

Because we hunger for God, we *will* find some place to eat. Whether it is in the Catholic Church, or down the street at World Victory Outreach Center, or up the street at Maranatha Faith Center, or across town at the First Baptist. You'll find a place to be fed. But the question remains: who really is feeding you? And what are you really being fed? How do you know you are being fed the entire Christ? How do you know that you are being offered the fullness of the Christian life?

God has made us to be in communion with Him and to know Him intimately. Is that what you are experiencing? Are you being fed the best of meals as a Christian? Now let's take a look and see what the Bible tells us about being fed, the One who feeds us, and how He has chosen to give Himself to us.

Chapter 3

Being Sheepish About Your Diet

What is the real hunger of your heart? A beautiful answer to this question is found in Psalm 23, the most famous of the 150 Psalms. Written by King David, a former shepherd, this psalm provides a perfect foundation for examining the theme and imagery of shepherding and sheep that runs through all of Scripture, as well as through this book. Here is Psalm 23:

> The Lord is my shepherd, I shall not want;
> He makes me lie down in green pastures.
>
> He leads me beside still waters; he restores my soul.
> He leads me in paths of righteousness for his name's sake.
>
> Even though I walk through the valley of the shadow of death,
> I fear no evil;
> For thou art with me; thy rod and thy staff, they comfort me.
>
> Thou preparest a table before me in the presence of my enemies;
> Thou anointest my head with oil, my cup overflows.
>
> Surely goodness and mercy shall follow me all the days of my life;
> And I shall dwell in the house of the Lord for ever.

Christians have long understood this psalm to refer, in a prophetic way, to Jesus. St. Augustine, in his commentary on Psalm 23, writes: "The Church speaks to Christ: 'The Lord feeds me, and I shall lack nothing' (verse 1). The Lord Jesus Christ is my Shepherd, 'and I shall lack nothing.'" Jesus, of course, is repeatedly presented throughout the New Testament as the Good Shepherd. He is described as the "Shepherd and Guardian of your souls" (1 Pt 2:25) and as the "Chief Shepherd" (1 Pt 5:4). There are many others places in the New Testament where the image of the sheep and their shepherd is used to describe the people (sometimes the Jews, sometimes the Church) and the person of Jesus.

The Life and Role of the Shepherd

The *Catechism* notes that "in Scripture, we find a host of interrelated images and figures through which Revelation speaks of the inexhaustible mystery of the Church" (CCC 753). One of the most common and striking images is taken "from the life of the shepherd." In order to appreciate these images and the connections between certain Old and New Testament passages in which they appear, we need to look at the life of a shepherd back in biblical times.

Going all the way back to the days of Abraham and the patriarchs, we find that nearly everyone in the nomadic families of that era was a shepherd and had a role in caring for the sheep. Sheep were at the heart of the nomadic life and were usually sheared twice a year. Sheep's wool was the most common material for clothing, since cotton was not available, linen was too expensive for most people, and camel's hair was far too rough (unless you were a prophet who ate locusts in the desert!). The sheep also produced milk, which was used to make cheese and butter. Sheep flesh was rarely eaten, and then only on feast days, such as the great feast of the Passover, or in honor of special guests.

The shepherd was responsible for tending the sheep and keeping them safe while leading them away from the camp or village to graze. Often he would have to move an entire flock single-handedly from one pasture to another, sometimes traveling miles in the process. The most important duty of the shepherd was to protect his flock. Everything else was secondary to making sure that none of his sheep got lost, injured themselves, or were killed by predators. In addition to guarding the sheep from wild animals, the shepherd also had to protect them from thieves and bad weather. Consequently the shepherd's work was never done; he worked continually, and often got little sleep.

The shepherd also had to find pasture for the sheep, and then move them safely to those locations. He knew the countryside intimately, as demonstrated by the story of David hiding in the wilderness from Saul for months on end. The shepherd would have to plan his movements with the sheep carefully; in the late fall and early winter there would be no pasture and he would have to give the sheep fodder. Because sheep don't like to drink from moving water, the shepherd would have to find quiet pools and lead them "beside still waters." When the water from the wild springs was dried up, the sheep would be fed from wells. The shepherd had no compass or watch or special equipment for finding his way; he had to memorize and know the land like the back of his work-worn, sun-tanned hand. If he needed shelter, he knew where caves were located; if he needed shade, he knew where the best grove of trees was found.

Lions, wolves, jackals, bears, and hyenas were the wild animals that a shepherd in the Holy Land might encounter. His weapons to ward them off were limited to a leather slingshot and a wooden club, sometimes with pieces of metal inserted into its top. The slingshot was very simple, consisting of two pieces of string and a piece of leather to hold the stone, the same sort of weapon used by David in killing Goliath (1 Sm 17:40-49). He would also carry a long rod, or staff, with a crook at one end. This was used to pull sheep out of tight spots, for climbing difficult terrain, and for guiding the sheep into the sheepfold, or pen, when necessary. The shepherd's clothing was modest: a plain cloak made of either leather or camel's hair, and leather sandals. He also had a *scrip*, a sort of knapsack, in which he carried bread, dates, cheese, raisins, and olives. Finally, the shepherd would sometimes carry a flute, used to brighten up the lonely evenings.

Sheep are not the most intelligent of animals, and so the shepherd's work could be exhausting and seemingly endless. Despite their mediocre intellect, however, the sheep could recognize the distinct call of the shepherd and the tone of his voice. When called, they immediately came running. When gathering the sheep to move on, the shepherd would call them; those who did not respond would sometimes get hit by a small pebble from the shepherd's slingshot. The relationship between the shepherd and his sheep was an intimate one. Not only could the shepherd call the sheep, he would name the sheep: "...and the sheep hear his voice, and he calls his own sheep by name, and leads them out" (Jn 10:3). He would have great affection for the sheep and would treat them with gentleness.

Unlike in the West, the Middle Eastern shepherd did not drive the sheep, but would lead them, walking in front, sometimes at the side. He walked at the rear of the flock only to gather up stragglers or to protect them from attacks by a lion or bear. This imagery is depicted by the prophet Isaiah: "But you will not go out in haste, Nor will you go as fugitives; For the Lord will go before you, And the God of Israel will be your rear guard" (Is 52:12). If a sheep was lost, the shepherd would spare no effort in finding it, even if it meant hours of searching, as Jesus' parable of the lost sheep describes:

> What man among you, if he has a hundred sheep and has lost one of them, does not leave the ninety-nine in the open pasture, and go after the one which is lost, until he finds it? And when he has found it, he lays it on his shoulders, rejoicing. And when he comes home, he calls together his friends and his neighbors, saying to them, "Rejoice with me, for I have found my sheep which was lost!" (Lk 15:4-6)

Though this parable certainly takes into consideration the great value of the lost sheep, the more important point is the reliability of the shepherd. Losing a sheep reflected badly on one's skills as a shepherd.

In crossing streams and rivers, the shepherd would watch carefully for any sheep struggling to get to the other side, grabbing those who might be swept away. Again, Isaiah uses this image in describing the relationship between God and His people: "When you pass through the waters, I will be with you; And through the rivers, they will not overflow you" (Is 43:2). The best shepherds would even risk their lives to keep their sheep from harm, demonstrating the sort of love spoken of by the Good Shepherd: "I am the good shepherd; the good shepherd lays down His life for the sheep" (Jn 10:11).

Jesus Christ, the Good Shepherd

This background and context helps us better appreciate the meaning of Psalm 23 and all the many passages of the New Testament that describe Jesus as the Good Shepherd. Knowing a bit about the life of David also helps us understand Psalm 23 and many of the other psalms written by him. David was a lowly shepherd boy when the prophet

Samuel anointed him as the King of Israel. A musician as well as a warrior, he wrote the majority of his psalms out in the Judean desert. Many of them were written while he was hiding from King Saul in the wilderness and in cities along the shore of the Dead Sea. Struggling with his desperate lifestyle and many worries, David was inspired to write psalms that convey the heart of God and still speak to people today, some three thousand years after they were written.

Because he was intimately acquainted with the desert, David knew better than anyone the dangers and problems faced in the rugged, desolate terrain. A primary concern was the lack of rain. It hardly rained at all, but when it did, tremendous flash floods gushed down into the Jordan Valley and instantly destroyed anything in their path. Because it didn't rain very much, there remained numerous well-worn trails and paths made by animals along the mountainsides and upon the desert plains. If you didn't know the land, you could easily get misled because of the multiple paths before you. And if you took the wrong path, you would soon be lost and end up miles from where you were supposed to be, or you could find yourself going in circles for days.

The good shepherd knew the paths and knew his sheep. His work—his very life—was to make certain his sheep followed the right paths and didn't go in the wrong direction. In Psalm 23, the word "path" can also be translated as "track." Jesus is the Good Shepherd who guides us in the tracks of righteousness. He knows the right path and He directs us towards it, even though we often stray away from it. "For you were continually straying like sheep," Peter writes, "but now you have returned to the Shepherd and Guardian of your souls" (1 Pt 2:25). How is it that we return? He searches for us and brings us back to Himself.

On our own, we starve and thirst. We get distracted. Like sheep, we are often helpless and foolish. The Shepherd of our souls wants to feed and guide us, but we don't always listen. But the people have to listen. It's like taking your kids shopping at the mall—you turn your head for one moment, and they're gone. One is heading for new clothes, another is hunting for music, and the third is making a beeline for the food court. How do you get their attention? You call their names. You're the one with the car keys and the purse strings. They think they are independent and don't need you, but they're wrong.

Similarly, Christians today are wandering all over the place. Some of them are heading toward one of the various denominational churches, and others are thinking about forming a non-denominational group of their own. It's all very complicated, messy, and confusing. Where do you go to hear the Word of God? Where do you go to get fed? Who do you decide to follow? Who will be your shepherd? There are many options, paths, and voices in the wilderness, all calling us to follow.

There are four major promises made in Psalm 23—four things that the Good Shepherd promises to do for His sheep who find themselves in the wilderness. Let's take a look at them:

The Good Shepherd leads and guides us into life:

> "He makes me lie down in green pastures. He leads me beside still waters; he restores my soul. He leads me in the paths of righteousness for his name's sake."

God became man in order to bring life to a dying world: "The thief comes only to steal, and kill, and destroy; I came that they might have life, and might have it abundantly" (Jn 10:10). Jesus knows the world and mankind better than any shepherd could ever know the wilderness or desert. He willingly took on the task of being the sole mediator between

God and man: "Jesus said to him, 'I am the way, and the truth, and the life; no one comes to the Father, but through me'" (Jn 14:6). This means that Jesus will provide for us, both physically and spiritually. He knows our needs even before we admit them to Him. Every sheep in His flock knows His voice, and He knows them all by name (Jn 10:3). His love and compassion for the sheep have no limits:

> He will feed his flock like a shepherd,
> He will gather the lambs in his arms,
> He will carry them in his bosom,
> And gently lead those that are with young (Is 40:11).

And why does He do this? Yes, because He loves us, but also because of His love for His Father. The Trinity is the reason for all that exists, for "God created the world for the sake of communion with his divine life" (CCC 760). He destined us to be His sons and daughters through Christ and to be conformed to the image of the Son, a plan "stemming immediately from Trinitarian love" (CCC 257). The eternal and perfect exchange of love between the Father, the Son, and the Holy Spirit are the reason that we exist, that the Son became man, that Jesus died on the Cross and rose again, and that now we are able to call God "*Abba!* Father!" It is for the Father's name's sake that, through the Holy Spirit, we are able to be Christ's namesakes— Christians.

The Good Shepherd saves us from evil and death:

> "Even though I walk through the valley of the shadow of death, I fear no evil; for thou art with me; thy rod and thy staff, they comfort me."

This verse brings to mind the great and perfect prayer given to us by Jesus, the Lord's Prayer, which asks of the Father, "And lead us not into temptation, but deliver us from evil." Because of His sacrificial death, Jesus the Good Shepherd has opened a way of life through the valley of the shadow of death. He has conquered the grave and death no longer is master over Him (Rom 6:9), nor over those who share in His life (see 1 Cor 15:55). The "great Shepherd of the sheep" has established an eternal covenant through His blood (Heb 13:20); He is also the High Priest of that covenant (see Heb 4-9).

In His wonderful parable of the Good Shepherd, Jesus says:

> Truly, truly, I say to you, I am the door of the sheep. All who came before me are thieves and robbers; but the sheep did not heed them. I am the door; if any one enters by me, he will be saved, and will go in and out and find pasture. The thief comes only to steal and kill and destroy; I came that they may have life, and have it abundantly. I am the good shepherd. The good shepherd lays down his life for the sheep. He who is a hireling and not a shepherd, whose own the sheep are not, sees the wolf coming and leaves the sheep and flees; and the wolf snatches them and scatters them. He flees because he is a hireling and cares nothing for the sheep. I am the good shepherd; I know my own and my own know me, as the Father knows me and I know the Father; and I lay down my life for the sheep (Jn 10:7-15).

The amazing thing is how Jesus chose to save us from death: He dies! "For this reason the Father loves me," He says, "because I lay down my life that I may take it up again" (Jn 10:17). How does the Shepherd eventually free humanity from sin and evil? He became a sheep. He is the High Priest and the sacrifice. He is both the Good Shepherd and the Passover Lamb. He is both God and man. He is both King of Kings and the Suffering Servant. He once came in humility and poverty, but He will come again in power and glory, finishing the conquering work He began on the Cross, when He defeated the powers of evil and darkness.

The Good Shepherd provides an eternal home, starting here on earth:

"Surely goodness and mercy shall follow me all the days of my life; and I shall dwell in the house of the Lord for ever."

Jesus has opened up the way to heaven for those who put their faith in His sacrificial offering and follow Him. But what sort of housing does He provide while we are still here on earth? According to Paul, the Church is our home in this life: "I write so that you may know how one ought to conduct himself in the household of God, which is the church of the living God, the pillar and support of the truth" (1 Tm 3:15). The Church is the house of the Lord, the place where the sheep gather together to worship and have communion with the Lamb. "The Church is, accordingly, a *sheepfold*," the *Catechism* explains, "the sole and necessary gateway to which is Christ. It is also the flock of which God Himself foretold that He would be the shepherd, and whose sheep, even though governed by human shepherds, are unfailingly nourished and led by Christ Himself, the Good Shepherd and Prince of Shepherds, who gave his life for his sheep" (CCC 754).

This might seem straightforward and simple enough, but as we will see in the next chapter, it isn't. As we've already seen, there are thousands of different groups and denominations claiming to be the correct path, guided by the Good Shepherd. So where *do* we find the one Church founded by Jesus? We start by looking to see who receives authority from Jesus to shepherd and guide His sheep. A big clue is given at the end of John's gospel, where Jesus has the following exchange with Peter, the head apostle, in the midst of the other apostles:

> When they had finished breakfast, Jesus said to Simon Peter, "Simon, son of John, do you love me more than these?" He said to him, "Yes, Lord; you know that I love you." He said to him, "Feed my lambs." A second time he said to him, "Simon, son of John, do you love me?" He said to him, "Yes, Lord; you know that I love you." He said to him, "Tend my sheep." He said to him the third time, "Simon, son of John, do you love me?" Peter was grieved because he said to him the third time, "Do you love me?" And he said to him, "Lord, you know everything; you know that I love you." Jesus said to him, "Feed my sheep" (Jn 21:15-17).

The apostles were all called to shepherd the flock formed by Jesus, but Peter was given a special position of authority in relation to that task. Just like Jesus, the apostles and their successors, the bishops of the Church, are called to lead and to guide, to feed and nourish, and to give up their lives for the sheep, if necessary. This is why Paul exhorts the bishops of Ephesus in this way: "Be on guard for yourselves and for all the flock, among which the Holy Spirit has made you overseers, to shepherd the church of God which He purchased with His own blood" (Acts 20:28).

The Good Shepherd anoints and gives food and drink:

> "Thou preparest a table before me in the presence of my enemies; thou anointest my head with oil, my cup overflows."

The Good Shepherd guides, protects, saves, and gives us a home and family. He also provides a family meal. This was prophesied by Ezekiel, who delivered these words from

God: "And I will set up over them one shepherd, my servant David, and he shall feed them: he shall feed them and be their shepherd" (Ez 34:23). Ezekiel wrote these words many years after the death of David. Did he expect David to be reincarnated? No, he expected a new son of David (Mt 1:1), who would re-establish God's rule and kingdom on earth. That son of David would be a ruler who would "shepherd my people Israel" (Mt 2:6; see Mi 5:2-4).

What is the food and drink that the Son of David will provide? Is it ordinary bread and wine? Is it food that merely *symbolizes* the great sacrifice of the Shepherd who is also the Passover Lamb? No, the food and drink on the table of God is the very body and blood of the Lamb of God: "Cleanse out the old leaven," Paul writes, "that you may be a new lump, as you really are unleavened. For Christ, our paschal lamb, has been sacrificed. Let us, therefore, celebrate the festival, not with the old leaven, the leaven of malice and evil, but with the unleavened bread of sincerity and truth" (1 Cor 5:7-8). The truth is that those anointed by the Holy Spirit (at baptism and confirmation) are invited to eat the life-giving flesh and blood of the Lamb. That's the point of John 6, and of the Last Supper accounts where we hear the words of Jesus: "Eat my flesh and drink my blood" and "This is my body" and "This is my blood."

In his grand vision of heaven described in the book of Revelation, St. John the Apostle sees Jesus, the Good Shepherd, at the right hand of the Father; He appears as "a Lamb standing, as if slain" (Rv 5:6). John then describes a great multitude of the saints coming out of the great tribulation on earth—the historical conflict between God and Satan. Their robes are washed and made "white in the blood of the Lamb" (Rv 7:14). These saved souls serve in the heavenly Temple and "they shall hunger no more, neither thirst any more; the sun shall not strike them, nor any scorching heat. For the Lamb in the midst of the throne will be their shepherd, and he will guide them to springs of living water; and God will wipe away every tear from their eyes" (Rv 7:16-17). The Eucharist is a foretaste of heaven, an anticipation of "the wedding feast of the Lamb in the heavenly Jerusalem" (CCC 1329). It is heavenly food, a supernatural feast. Heaven is the fulfillment of the Eucharist, the unveiling of the Communion that on earth is hidden by the appearance of bread and wine.

Finding the Shepherd's Sheepfold

As a Protestant pastor, I thought that I had everything. I had green pastures and still waters—or so it seemed for many years. But something was missing. For many years I denied the fact that my table was not prepared and my cup did not overflow. Yes, I had a great job, a beautiful family, and a comfortable home. But I began to hear the Good Shepherd calling me to a place I feared to go. I had no choice but to follow Him, even though it meant walking on narrow paths and steep mountains. It meant trusting Jesus, who knows the desert of life and the wilderness of our souls better than anyone else ever can.

There were many paths that I could have taken; many trails that would have led somewhere else. But the path He led me on took me back home to the house of the Lord, the altar of the Lamb, and the Blessed Sacrament. I now want to tell you about some of those other paths in the wilderness and explain why the path Jesus wants to lead each of us down is the one leading to the One, Holy, Catholic, and Apostolic Church. I now want to set out why the Catholic Church is where you will be fed the meal that God desires for every one of His children.

Chapter 4

Options In The Desert

If you venture into the desert you soon see that there are hundreds, even thousands, of paths. Trails lead in every possible direction, but you find no signs indicating which way to go. Religiously, the number of possibilities can make your head spin: Baptist, Pentecostal, Methodist, Lutheran, Mormon, Jehovah's Witness, Presbyterian, Four Square, Episcopalian, Greek Orthodox—the list goes on and on. What is a seeker to do?

The Trails of Broken Communion

Perhaps you believe that Jesus established a *single* Church and that one of these trails must lead to it. You therefore search for the oldest trail—the one that has been there for two thousand years. As you search, though, you may be surprised at the number of options that faced even the earliest Christians.

In the first century, just years after Jesus ascended into heaven, a number of tracks and trails were presented to those who professed faith in Christ. Already there were people within the Church who rebelled against the authority of the apostles and demanded that they, not the Church, be recognized as having the fullness of truth.

One tempting trail was blazed by the Judaizers, who insisted that, in order to be true followers of the Messiah, Christians had to follow every jot and tittle of the Mosaic Law. Any Christian who didn't keep all of the commandments and follow every single dietary law was not considered one of the truly spiritual and knowledgeable followers of Christ. Paul, himself a former rabbi, spent much time and effort dealing with Judaizers, trying to get them to see that salvation is by grace and not by works of the law. On the other side were Christians who were still attached to their pagan pasts and had a difficult time letting go of beliefs that weren't compatible with the faith of the Church. They tended to fall back into lifestyles that were scandalous to their fellow believers (see 1 Cor 5).

By the second century, matters became even more complicated. The emergence of Gnosticism proved to be one the most dangerous false beliefs (or *heresies*), because the Gnostics were adept at using Christian terminology to talk about beliefs that weren't Christian at all. They were the forerunners of today's New Agers, who might talk highly of Jesus and His divinity, but also insist that all of us are just as divine as Jesus as long as we tap into our "Christ-consciousness" and "God potential." The Docetist Gnostics believed that Jesus and "the Christ" were two different persons, and that the true Christ was spirit only, not flesh. They believed that the Jesus who died on the Cross was merely a physical vessel for the Christ. This falsehood was based on the Docetist belief that the material, physical realm was evil and corrupt, and that salvation was found in escaping from the body and by spiritually ascending through the "heavenlies." The same basic idea is embraced by a bewildering number of groups today, including the Church of Scientology and Christian Science.

Then there were the Montanists, who focused almost exclusively on the Holy Spirit and attached great importance to prophesying, speaking in tongues, and experiencing ecstasies. Their trail naturally led into anti-authoritarian territory, where truth is discovered through private revelation and through prophets who aren't in communion with the Church founded by Jesus. This trail was based on experience and emotion; it had little use for logic and discernment.

In the fourth century, the Church faced an even bigger problem with Arianism, the belief that Jesus, though divine, was not equal to God the Father, but was a lesser god who was created at a particular moment in time. The Church spent most of the fourth century fighting against this seductive belief, and it is estimated that at one point more than two-thirds of the world's bishops embraced some form of Arianism. Today, a type of Arianism is taught by several groups, most notably the Watchtower Society, better known as the Jehovah's Witnesses.

There were many other perilous trails in the early Church: Sabellianism, Nestorianism, Apollinarianism, Eutychianism, Monothelitism, Modalism, and Pelagianism. Many of these heresies had to do with the nature or person of Jesus Christ. People were struggling with big questions: Who exactly was Jesus? If He was the Son of God, was He equal to God the Father? Did He have one nature or two? Was He one Person or two? Was He more God than man or more man than God? These vital issues would be addressed in the first several ecumenical councils, beginning with the Council of Nicea in A.D. 325.

Throughout those first few centuries there were the Church fathers, courageous men who fought to preserve the Faith passed on to them by Jesus and His apostles. Among them were: Clement of Rome, the fourth pope, who chastised the Corinthians for not behaving like Christians; Ignatius of Antioch, a bishop evidently acquainted with some of the apostles, who during his journey to martyrdom in Rome exhorted the churches along his route to hold fast to the apostolic faith and follow the leadership of the bishops; and Irenaeus of Lyon, an apologist who tirelessly fought against the Gnostics and described in his writings how the true faith and the Christian way of life were handed down from generation to generation (i.e., Sacred Tradition).

Although bishops and leaders throughout the Christian world fought against such false teachings, a break between the Western and Eastern Churches was already developing in those early centuries. The challenge of different languages and cultures, coupled with political alignments, began to take its toll. Less than a century into the second Christian millennium, these tensions resulted in a *schism* ("split" or "division") between the West and East. Although there had been many small trails (i.e., heretical movements) to follow prior to this sad event, the wanderer in the desert now had two major trails to choose from: the Roman Catholic Church and the Eastern Orthodox Churches.

Within a few centuries of this division, new challenges began developing in the West. In the late 1300s, John Wycliffe, a professor of theology at Oxford University in England, began to question the authority of the Church and to doubt some of its central teachings, including the belief in the Real Presence in the Eucharist. Not long after, the Bohemian preacher John Hus took up some of Wycliffe's doctrines and carried them even further. The fact that some of the clergy—including a number of popes—were either morally corrupt or poorly educated didn't help matters and led to further unrest and confusion.

In 1517, an Augustinian monk named Martin Luther nailed his *95 Theses* to the church door at Wittenberg, Germany, setting off the Protestant Reformation. Following right on Luther's heels were John Calvin in Geneva, the founder of the Reformed tradition of Protestantism, and the former Swiss priest Ulrich Zwingli, who led the more radically-minded Protestants. More and more trails began to appear and confusion among the sheep was rampant, with new leaders and voices and beliefs appearing on a regular basis. Soon, the Church in England split from the Catholic Church because King Henry VIII wanted a divorce. Thereafter, English Catholics were severely persecuted, driven underground, and even martyred.

Between the 1500s and the beginning of the 20th century, it is estimated that close to 2,000 new tracks were created: Lutheran, Calvinist, Anabaptist, Anglican, Methodist, Baptist, Puritan, Plymouth Brethren, Seventh-day Adventism, and many more. The desert was filled with the clamor of emerging groups, movements, beliefs, leaders, and self-proclaimed shepherds. One trail led to Pentecostalism, another to Fundamentalism, this one to liberal Protestantism, and that one to conservative Evangelicalism. So many trails, so many options—what is a sheep to do?

As mentioned earlier, a recent edition of the *World Christian Encyclopedia* lists more than 33,000 Christian denominations, not including "non-denominational" denominations. The question for the average believer is who do we follow? Which one will truly feed us? All churches and denominations claim they are the true trail. Each says that it has the best meal. Almost all of them claim to base their beliefs on "Scripture alone," even though they have different teachings on specific issues, often based on the same biblical passages.

Which of the Endless Answers Is Correct?

The sheep are hungry and needy. Where will they go?

There are so many questions the sheep must ask as they gaze upon the criss-crossing trails in front of, behind, and beside them: What is baptism? What does it do? Does it require sprinkling or immersion? Is it needed at all? What about marriage? Is it a sacrament? Who or what group interprets the Bible? Which translation of the Bible is reliable?

There are even bigger questions, similar to the ones the early Church had to address. Who is Jesus? A great teacher? A political revolutionary? The Son of God? Did He really die and then rise from the dead? Did He really found a Church? What about the Eucharist? Does bread and wine really become the body and blood of Christ or is it just a symbol? Is bread and wine required or will crackers and grape juice suffice? How often should the Eucharist be celebrated? Who can receive it? Who cannot?

Martin Luther had a strong devotion to the Eucharist, believing that it truly did contain the body and blood of Christ, although he also believed that the essence of the bread and wine still remained.

John Calvin believed that the Eucharist was a symbol of Christ's body with great spiritual power, but that the elements were not changed in any way. Speaking of Luther's devotion to the Eucharist, Calvin stated, that "He has sinned" and was acting "from ignorance and the grossest extravagance." Luther's view, Calvin stated, was "a very foul error" full of "absurdities."

Zwingli went even further, insisting that the Eucharist was only a symbol and nothing more. The Swiss reformer believed the same was true of baptism. In his view, the sacraments have no power and cannot convey God's grace. This was logical to a certain extent, since the Reformers generally agreed that grace was God's external favor only—not the actual Trinitarian life of God, who desires to dwell in us and transform us, as Catholics and Eastern Orthodox Christians believe.

By the end of the sixteenth century, there were literally dozens of different beliefs about the Eucharist and the meaning of Jesus' words, "Eat my flesh and drink my blood."

Just sixty years after the posting of Martin Luther's *95 Theses*, a book was published in Ingolstadt, Germany, entitled *Two Hundred Interpretations of the Words, "This Is My Body"* (see Fr. John Hardon's *A Catholic Catechism*, p. 461). Imagine how many interpretations you would find for these words today!

A person can begin to despair, wondering if there really are answers to these critically important questions. Finding the answers is often too formidable a task for the average believer. The complexity of the topics, combined with the average believer's limited theological education, causes many to dismiss the idea of objective truth with phrases such as "Jesus is the important thing, and we'll just agree to disagree on all the rest," or "I like the way so and so teaches, it just *feels* right."

During my twelve years as a pastor, I would often stay up late on Saturday night preparing my sermon for the next day. I used to pore over many Bible passages, trying to come up with something to feed the people in my congregation, all the while wondering in the back of my mind, "Am I right? Am I sure? Do I really have the correct answer? What if I'm wrong and the Lutherans are right? What if the Methodists have the inside track on this issue?" I knew that I was going to have to stand before God and answer for what I taught from the pulpit. How could I know for sure that I was right? And if I was right, what about everyone else? Were all the other churches and denominations wrong?

This is the dilemma faced by Christians today. It is especially faced by Protestants, who are sincerely looking for the fullness of truth, but aren't certain that they have it. I know of wonderful Evangelicals who have stopped attending church, sometimes for months or years at a time, because they gave up on finding a group that teaches everything correctly. And yet they aren't even sure if *they* are correct on everything. The desert dust is swirling and they are half-blinded by the winds and the heat. Where is the Shepherd? Which trail does He want them to travel down?

"I Am the Good Shepherd"

In the tenth chapter of John's gospel we find some answers to these fundamental questions, truths that prepare us to see more clearly the path the Good Shepherd is pointing out to us. In John 10:11, Jesus speaks about Himself and says, "I am the Good Shepherd, the Shepherd lays down his life for the sheep." This point is so important that He immediately repeats it: "I am the good shepherd; and I know my own, and my own know me, even as the Father knows me and I know the Father; and I lay down my life for the sheep" (Jn 10:14-15).

Jesus has the ultimate responsibility as the Shepherd of our souls. He has taken his stance and said, "I am your Shepherd. I love you. I will feed you. I will protect you. I will guide you." He is always there for us and wants what is best for us. He wants to lead us.

So why is there so much confusion? Why are there so many trails?

One reason is that there are thieves who come to steal, kill, and destroy (Jn 10:10). This refers to those who willfully misuse and abuse the teachings of Jesus for their own gain. These include the cult leaders, corrupt televangelists, and abusive clergy. They create confusion and destroy lives.

Another reason that there are so many trails is that sincere people are often sincerely wrong. Like Luther, Calvin, or Zwingli, they become so focused on one or two issues, they lose sight of the big picture. They end up throwing out the baby with the bath water. Luther reacted against certain abuses within the hierarchy and ended up going way too far. Among other things, he decided to add the word "alone" to the phrase "For we maintain that a man is justified by faith apart from works of the Law" (Rom 3:28), buttressing his sincere, but incorrect, belief that salvation is by "faith alone." The history of Christianity is filled with sincere yet misguided actions, usually carried out by people who love Jesus and believe that they are following His every word and command.

Catholics agree with Protestants about *who* Jesus Christ is. He is the Good Shepherd; He is Lord and Savior; He is God. But the next issue is *how*: How is Jesus going to feed us? How is He going to lead us? How is He going to protect and guide us? We agree that Jesus is the Way, the Truth, and the Life, but how does He show us the Way, how does He convey the Truth, and how does He share His life with us? Is it through the Church? If so, which church?

We'll examine these questions in detail a little further on. Right now, however, we need to point out that many people don't want to hear the answer to the *how* question. They are unwilling to take the claims of the Catholic Church seriously. "It's full of scandals and corruption," they say, "How could Jesus' Church have so many problems?" Yes, the Church is made up of sinners; in fact, it is a hospital for sinners and often looks and smells like a hospital, with ill patients, raw wounds, and disease on every side. Such things bother us and make us uncomfortable, but where else are the wounded and dying to go? They would pass out and die in the desert alongside the dusty trails.

True, there are problems in the Church today. There were problems in the Church 2,000 years ago as well, as Paul's letters to the Corinthians clearly show. But, through all scandals and difficulties, Jesus manages to feed us because He is the Good Shepherd and is true to His promises. We rely on His ability to feed us, not on the cleverness or eloquence of men.

Imagine how the disciples must have felt. In the tenth chapter of John's Gospel, Jesus had given an encouraging talk about how He protects, guides, and feeds His sheep. But, soon thereafter, while celebrating Passover with them, He tells them that He will be leaving soon. They look at each other in dismay. "What do you mean, Lord?" I can hear them objecting: "Why, Lord?"

Jesus reassures them: "And when I go and prepare a place for you, I will come again and will take you to myself, that where I am you may be also" (Jn 14:3). Isn't that comforting? Jesus said, "I will receive you to myself!" So many people that I talk to are searching those many paths out there in the desert. They ask, "What does this one teach? What's does that one have to say? What is he offering today? Why should I go to his church?" They are looking, searching, yearning to find answers. But, Jesus said, "*I* will come to *you*" (Jn 14:18).

This brings us back to the big question: *how*? How will Jesus come to us and receive us to Himself? Did Jesus give us His teaching and then leave, saying, "Figure it out. I'll be praying for you"? Did He intend that the individual Christian should have to discover truth for himself? Did He say that whatever we teach is fine as long as we believe two or three essential things? No, Jesus states that He will send a supernatural counselor: "And I will pray the Father, and He will give you another Counselor, to be with you for ever" (Jn 14:16). This counselor is the Holy Spirit, the Spirit of truth, the Lord and Giver of Life. He will be sent in the name of Jesus, just as the Son was sent by the will of the Father. This is Trinitarian love in action.

And what will the Holy Spirit do? "He will teach you all things, and bring to your remembrance all that I have said to you" (Jn 14:26). To whom does Jesus say this: to you and me? No, to His apostles, the same men (minus Judas) to whom Jesus gives this great commission shortly before His ascension into heaven: "All authority in heaven and on earth has been given to me. Go therefore and make disciples of all nations, baptizing them in the name of the Father and of the Son and of the Holy Spirit, teaching them to observe all that I have commanded you; and lo, I am with you always, to the close of the age" (Mt 28:18-20).

Chapter 5

Will The Real Authority Please Stand Up?

Scripture Was Never Meant to Fly Sola

We need to take a moment and look at the fundamental Protestant belief in *sola scriptura* ("Scripture alone") because it is so important to this discussion. In fact, much in this book hinges on the question, "Who is the final authority for the Christian?" *Sola scriptura* is a belief that I held dearly as a Protestant; it was as essential to me as breathing and eating. But I finally recognized, reluctantly, that Jesus never committed His teachings to writing and then said, "Good luck interpreting them! Just try to get along." No, He had a group of apostles whom He taught and trained and established as the leaders of His Church. These were the men who would proclaim the Gospel and feed the sheep with the bread from heaven.

Through hard experience and careful study, I became convinced that the Bible does not state, either explicitly or implicitly, that it is the sole authority when it comes to the Christian Faith. *Sola scriptura* is not found, in any form, in the Bible. Twelve years of experience as the pastor of a congregation taught me that most Protestants don't actually follow a "Scripture alone" approach in many real-life situations. *Sola scriptura* sounds great until you actually have to live the Christian life. Decisions and interpretations must be made about many things, including many difficult and confusing passages of Scripture. So while anti-Catholics attack the teaching authority of Peter and his successors, they do so based on their *own* authority as the final judge of Scripture. In reality this means that they have set themselves up as pope!

Monsignor Ronald Knox was a brilliant Anglican priest and author who converted to Catholicism. In his wonderful book, *The Belief of Catholics,* Knox summarizes perfectly the problems with the "Scripture alone" argument:

> The Church, for Catholics, is a visible fact; for Protestants it is an intellectual figment. ...The Bible, it appeared, was common ground between the combatants. The Bible, therefore, was the arena of the struggle; from it the controversialist, like David at the brook, must pick up texts to sling at his adversary. In fact, of course, the Protestant had no conceivable right to base any arguments on the inspiration of the Bible. For the inspiration of the Bible was a doctrine which had been believed, before the Reformation, on the mere authority of the Church; it rested on exactly the same basis as the doctrine of Transubstantiation. Protestantism repudiated Transubstantiation, and in doing so repudiated the authority of the Church; and then, without a shred of logic, calmly went on believing in the inspiration of the Bible, as if nothing had happened! Did they suppose that Biblical inspiration was a self-evident fact, like the axioms of Euclid? Or did they derive it from some words of our Lord? If so, what words? What authority have we, apart from that of the Church, to say that the Epistles of Paul are inspired, and the Epistle of Barnabas is not?

Knox's summary touches on a number of difficulties facing the "Bible-only" believer. First, a unified, established Church existed *before* the New Testament was written. The early Christians gathered around the apostles' teaching, first in its oral form and then in both oral and written form. Paul mentions that he persecuted the Church (1 Cor 15:9; Gal

1:13), meaning that the Church was in existence before Paul became a Christian, let alone an author of inspired epistles.

Second, the New Testament books were written by men with apostolic authority granted to them by Christ. The Bible, inspired by the Holy Spirit, came *through the Church* via the apostles, chosen to be the instruments of authority within the body of Christ (see Luke 10:16; 1 Cor 12:28).

Third, the twenty-seven books that are in the New Testament canon were chosen by the Catholic Church, specifically by the bishops, the successors of the apostles. It was the Church, through the apostolic authority given it by Jesus that vouched for the authenticity and inspiration of those books.

Fourth, the process by which the canon was formed and finalized took place over a long period of time. Certain books, such as the book of Revelation, were not fully accepted until the third and fourth centuries.

Fifth, the process of discerning whether or not a book is part of the canon was similar to the type of development of thought that resulted in authoritative decisions about the Incarnation, the Trinity, and a multitude of other theological issues. These decisions followed a certain pattern: First, a controversy would arise about a theological question. A lengthy period of time would usually follow, sometimes years long, during which bishops and theologians would discuss, argue, and debate. Eventually a council would be convened and an authoritative definition would be made. This has been the pattern of the Church from its earliest days, beginning with the Council of Jerusalem (see Acts 15).

Knox rightly points out the irony of the Protestant position. Until the Protestant Reformation, no one thought that the books in the New Testament belonged there because the books themselves said so (since they clearly do not) or because they claimed to be the Word of God. Many of them, such as

Philemon, 2 and 3 John, and Jude are rather puzzling entries in the canon, as they lack any significant doctrinal teachings. In addition, there were many Christian writings in existence in the first three centuries, many bearing the names of various apostles, such as the gospel of Peter, the gospel of James, etc. Who decided whether or not they belonged in the canon? We might say that a book had to be "orthodox" in its teaching, but who had the authority to determine what was "orthodox"?

A Catholic sees the Church as a living body, the Body of Christ, who is guardian and interpreter of Scripture. Throughout 2,000 years of history the teachings of the Church have never contradicted the Bible; they have only contradicted some people's interpretations of the Bible. While Protestants may say, "The Scripture is the only teacher I need—all truth is there," thousands of denominations show the consequences of such a subjective (albeit sincere) mentality.

To put it differently, Fundamentalists and Evangelicals generally believe that the Bible is complete in itself. Anything not found in its pages is seen as the work of human interest, or even pagan corruption, whether it is called "tradition" or "development." This idea is the bedrock for those assemblies that call themselves "New Testament" churches, which claim that they "worship and live just like the early Church." If they strictly adhered to the idea that the Bible is complete in itself and self-interpreting, they would not believe the Lord's Supper to be merely symbolic or baptism is merely testimonial in nature because the Bible says otherwise. Nor would they use the terms *trinity* or *incarnation* (and, more importantly, understand them as they do). Terms such as *trinity* are not explicitly stated in the Bible; they were codified over time by the Church as a clarification of its Sacred Tradition.

Catholics are often criticized by some Protestants for beliefs such as transubstantiation or various Marian doctrines because they have no explicit biblical evidence. Yet these same critics fail to live up to their own standards. For it is not as clear as they think that certain beliefs which they hold are true or evident from the Bible alone, such as the divinity of the Holy Spirit or the equality of the Son with the Father. And the clincher is that their core belief—that the Bible contains all revealed truth and it alone is authoritative—is itself not found in the Bible!

Take, for instance, the proof text used by those who hold to *sola scriptura*, 2 Timothy 3:16: "All scripture is inspired by God and profitable for teaching, for reproof, for correction, and for training in righteousness." While this text certainly declares the great importance of Scripture, it certainly does not communicate that the Bible is the *only* source of divine revelation. And, since the New Testament had not yet been written at this point, the "scripture" that St. Paul is referring to is the Old Testament. So if we use this passage as a proof text to defend "scripture alone" as our authority, then we really only need the Old Testament.

When I studied these matters as a Protestant pastor, I began to understand why I rarely made mention of the first fifteen centuries of Christian writing, thought, and theology in my teaching. In many instances, what I believed as a Protestant pastor did not line up well with the writings of the Church fathers, Scholastic theologians, and great mystics, not to mention the decrees of the popes and the ecumenical councils. My belief in *sola scriptura* painted me into a tight corner: If I really were a "Bible only" believer I would have no problem throwing away all the developments in doctrine that transpired after the first century. But I couldn't do that without throwing out the canon of the Bible, the Trinity, and many other essential beliefs.

I Like Upholding the Family Tradition

It is not an exaggeration to say that most Fundamentalists and Evangelicals dislike and even despise what Catholics understand as Sacred Tradition. Such critics mock Tradition, believing it to be "unbiblical" and even spiritually dangerous. They confuse the "traditions of men" with the divinely-revealed Tradition of the Church. Yet the Bible itself speaks positively of Tradition in more than one place. Paul writes to the believers at Thessalonica: "So then, brethren, stand firm and hold to the traditions which you were taught by us, either by word of mouth or by letter" (2 Thess 2:15). And to Timothy, Paul's writes: "You then, my son, be strong in the grace that is in Christ Jesus, and what you have *heard* from me before many witnesses entrust to faithful men who will be able to teach others also" (2 Tm 2:1-2, emphasis added).

Anti-Catholic Protestants insist that Jesus spoke against tradition and labeled it evil and to be avoided. But the Gospels show that Jesus makes a distinction between God-given tradition and tradition that is merely human. In Matthew 15:1-9, Jesus condemns the Jewish tradition of *Korban*, the avoidance of giving financial support to one's parents by declaring the money to be dedicated to God, because it is contrary to the commandment to honor father and mother. But in the same Gospel Jesus says to the people: "The scribes and the Pharisees have seated themselves in the chair of Moses; therefore all that they tell you, do and observe, but do not do according to their deeds, for they say things and do not do them" (Mt 23:2-3). Here Jesus acknowledges the authority of the Jewish leaders, but condemns their hypocrisy. He does not attack tradition *per se*, but only the cynical and hypocritical emptiness of the leader's actions.

It makes little sense to hold that the New Testament presents in finished form every bit of theological truth. Most of the epistles in the New Testament were "occasional" in nature, written to address a specific circumstance or event, typically to reprimand or encourage a local church or to provide guidance in difficult matters. It goes without saying that the churches established at Corinth, Ephesus, Antioch, and Galatia had already learned the traditions of the apostles pertaining to the ordinary, daily life of the churches (see 1 Cor 11:23; 2 Thess 2:15). Teachings about the liturgy, the sacraments, and church would have been passed on orally, that is, by word of mouth.

This reliance on oral tradition makes sense, given that the first epistle of the New Testament wasn't written until about A.D. 49-55, some twenty years after Jesus' ascension into heaven. And there would have been only a handful of copies in existence, since each one had to be transcribed by hand. Consequently the common believer certainly did not possess copies of the New Testament books. Thus, from the very start of the Church, a vibrant oral tradition existed that was passed along from church to church, believer to believer.

Many "Bible Christians" insist that Catholic Tradition began to develop in the fourth century, after Christianity was made the official religion of the Roman Empire. But the reality of an established apostolic Tradition existed centuries before then. The great theologian Irenaeus, who lived from A.D. c.130-200 and combated Gnosticism, wrote the following in his masterwork, *Against Heresies*:

> Yet when we appeal again to that tradition which is derived from the Apostles, and which is safeguarded in the churches through the succession of presbyters, they then are adversaries of tradition, claiming to be wiser not only than the presbyters [priests] but even than the Apostles, and to have discovered the truth undefiled...Thus it comes about that they now agree neither with the Scriptures nor with tradition...Those who wish to discern the truth may observe the apostolic tradition made manifest in every church throughout the world. We can enumerate those who were appointed bishops in the churches by the Apostles, and their successors down to our own day...[we point] to the apostolic tradition and the faith that is preached to men, which has come down to us through the succession of bishops; the tradition and creed of the greatest, the most

> ancient church, the church known to all men, which was founded and set up at Rome by the two most glorious Apostles, Peter and Paul. For with this church, because of its position of leadership and authority, must needs agree every church, that is, the faithful everywhere; for in her the apostolic tradition has always been preserved by the faithful from all parts.

Irenaeus did not appeal to the written Scripture alone, but to Tradition and the authority of the apostles, passed on to their successors. He makes it clear that only those churches and leaders in communion with the Church of Rome were considered to be in right fellowship and part of the universal body of Christ. As we will see, it was the Church of Rome, led by the Bishop of Rome, that held a special place in the early Church—and for one simple reason: Jesus chose Peter to be *the Rock*.

Chapter 6

Who Do *You* Say Jesus Is?

Matthew 16:18-19 is a passage with which many Catholics are familiar, for it contains Jesus' famous words to Peter:

> And I tell you, you are Peter, and on this rock I will build my church, and the powers of death shall not prevail against it. I will give you the keys of the kingdom of heaven, and whatever you bind on earth shall be bound in heaven, and whatever you loose on earth shall be loosed in heaven.

This is a powerful statement deserving careful interpretation. First, however, we need to examine a part of this passage that is sometimes overlooked: the question and answer immediately prior to Peter's declaration and Jesus' granting of authority.

A Question of Mistaken Identity

Having taken His disciples outside of Judea into the district of Caesarea Philippi (Mt 16:13), Jesus asks them this question, "Who do men say that the Son of Man is?"

In his 14th homily on the gospel of Matthew, the great Father of the Church, St. John Chrysostom, has this to say about Jesus' remarkable question: "Note that Jesus does not raise this question at the beginning of His preaching but only after He had done many miracles, had talked through with them many lofty teachings, and had given them many clear proofs of His divinity and of His union with the Father. Only then does He put this question to them."

Like the people who have followed Jesus throughout His ministry, the disciples have heard the Sermon on the Mount, they have seen Jesus heal people who are sick and lame and mute, and they have seen the five thousand fed with just two loaves and five fish.

It is obvious from Jesus' encounter with the Pharisees and Sadducees in Matthew 16:1-12 what the religious leaders of the day thought of Jesus. But what did the people think? Who did *they* say Jesus was? In verse 14, we hear their responses: "John the Baptist ... Elijah ... Jeremiah ... one of the prophets." One question, four answers, and all the answers were wrong! Yet the people had seen the miracles and had heard Jesus speak with authority. They had looked Him in the face and eaten bread and fish miraculously produced at His hands by His blessing. And they still didn't know Who He is. The people had touched the God-man and had been fed by Him but did not recognize Him (see Jn 1; 1 Jn 1-4).

Now let's be honest: would we have done much better? I seriously doubt it, especially since there are thousands of biblical scholars and students who study the Bible for years and conclude that Jesus was simply a traveling preacher with a big heart and a message of love, or an apocalyptic visionary who was confused about His own identity, or a reforming prophet who ended up on the wrong side of a complex religious conflict.

I've even heard of biblical scholars who are agnostics. Obviously God did not intend for people to sit alone with their Bibles and figure out the entire Christian Faith on their own. Is that how it happened at the Council of Nicea? Is that how it worked in the early Church? Irenaeus tells us that the heretics also appealed to Scripture, pointing out that we need a divinely-given interpreter of Scripture: the Church founded by Christ. In other words, how can we trust our interpretation of the Bible and trust that the Bible is true and accurate, but turn away from the Church that defended, protected, and defined the canon of the Bible?

When it comes to knowing the Good Shepherd as He wishes to be known, we need more than our own reflection and ideas, good as they might be. We need the supernatural, gracious guidance of Christ. He is the Shepherd, who promised to come to us, lead us, and feed us. So it is not a choice between having an individual relationship with Jesus *or* being part of the Church. It's both.

Strictly limiting yourself to one or the other would be like getting married and saying to your spouse, "Your family means nothing to me; I want nothing to do with them. I just want you." When you marry, you marry into the entire family. And to really know your spouse, you need to know his or her family. To really know Who Jesus is, you need to belong to His "family"—His Body—the Church that He founded.

A Rock-Solid Answer

For those who come to theological conclusions by putting their finger in the air to test the various options, Jesus gives us an example by first asking the Apostles what others think of him. Notice that all their answers were wrong. How often do we look to the opinion of others rather than seek out His authority for answers? Knowing that the Father would reveal the correct answer, Jesus asks them the most important question, "But who do *you* say that I am?" (v. 15).

Peter steps up and answers, "Thou art the Christ, the Son of the Living God." Jesus then responds, "Blessed are you, Simon Bar-Jona! For flesh and blood has not revealed this to you, but my Father who is in heaven. And I tell you, you are Peter, and on this rock I will build my church, and the powers of death shall not prevail against it" (Mt 16:17-18). It's not surprising that, years later, Peter would write these words of warning: "But know this first of all, that no prophecy of Scripture is a matter of one's own interpretation, for no prophecy was ever made by an act of human will, but men moved by the Holy Spirit spoke from God" (2 Pt 1:20-21). Peter knew from personal experience the highs and lows of being a disciple; he knew very well that trust in the Holy Spirit was essential if believers are to stay grounded in the truth.

Peter (*Petros*) is the rock (*petra*). This play on the word "rock" and the use of the feminine form *petra* in Greek has led some Protestants to deny that Peter is the rock. They say that Jesus is the only rock, or that Peter's faith is the rock (as if Peter could be separated from his faith!). But other Protestant scholars have acknowledged that Jesus is clearly designating Peter the rock upon which He will build His Church. For example, noted Protestant biblical scholar D.A. Carson, writing in *The Expositor's Bible Commentary*, explains that

> the underlying Aramaic [in Matthew 16:18] is in this case unquestionable; and most probably *kepha* [the Aramaic word for "rock"] was used in both clauses ("you are *kepha*" and "on this *kepha*"), since the word was used both for a name and for a "rock." . . . The Greek makes a distinction between *petros* and *petra* simply because it is trying to preserve the original pun, and in Greek the feminine name *petra* could not very well serve as a masculine name.

In having his name changed by God, Peter joins a list of people that includes Abram, Jacob, and Saul. All of these men were specially chosen for roles of leadership, a fact demonstrated by their name change. And the name "Peter" (*Kepha*) given to him by Jesus (Jn 1:42), was unique among Jews. In fact, it was not used for humans because only God was referred to as "Rock" (see Dt 32:4,18; 2 Sam 22:47; Ps 89:26) And yet Jesus calls Peter a "rock," and it was upon this flawed, impetuous, and stubborn fisherman that Jesus chose to build His Church. The *Catechism* explains:

> The Lord made Simon alone, whom he named Peter, the "rock" of his Church. He gave him the keys of his Church and instituted him shepherd of the whole flock. "The office of binding and loosing which was given to Peter was also assigned to the college of apostles united to its head." [*Lumen gentium* 22.2]. This pastoral office of Peter and the other apostles belongs to the Church's very foundation and is continued by the bishops under the primacy of the Pope (CCC 881).

Peter, Peter, Kingdom Leader

The role of Peter can only be ignored if a person is willing to throw out entirely the biblical claims that the Catholic Church makes about his authority. Peter heads nearly every list of the apostles (see Mt 10:1-4; Mk 3:16-19, among others) and he almost always spoke (sometimes rashly) for them as well. Peter was a prominent figure in key New Testament events such as Jesus' walking on the water, the miraculous catch of fish, the confrontation with the authorities in the Garden, the preaching at Pentecost, the first healing after Pentecost, receiving the revelation that Gentiles were to be baptized, and having the position of honor at the Council of Jerusalem. All told, Peter is mentioned in more than sixty different contexts in the four Gospels, while no one else garners more than twenty-five mentions. And he is the only person ever specifically blessed by Jesus: "Blessed are you, Simon" (Mt 16:17). Regardless of how one interprets Matthew 16, it is clear that Peter is singled out in some manner and for some purpose.

What was that purpose? To hold the keys of the kingdom of heaven and to bind and loose. Why keys? In Jewish culture keys were a sign of royalty, ownership, and authority. These keys are symbols of the office of the prime minister, who was the highest of the twelve officials, or deputies, over Israel (1 Kgs 4:7) in the Davidic kingdom. This position is spoken of in Isaiah 22 in reference to Eliakim:

> And I will clothe him with your tunic, and tie your sash securely about him, I will entrust him with your authority, and he will become a father to the inhabitants of Jerusalem and to the house of Judah. Then I will set the key of the house of David on his shoulder, when he opens no one will shut, when he shuts no one will open. And I will drive him like a peg in a firm place, and he will become a throne of glory to his father's house" (Is 22:21-23).

The vicar, or prime minister, would oversee the kingdom while the King was away. And he would wield the keys to the Kingdom until the King returned for them (see Rv 1:18). This authority given by Christ to Peter does not guarantee sinlessness (*impeccability*); Peter remains a human being capable of sin. What it does guarantee is that in matters of dogma and doctrine the Holy Spirit will keep Peter and his successors from teaching error, which is called *infallibility*. This is not a license to create doctrine; it is a *negative protection*—that is, it keeps the pope from teaching anything false.

In rabbinical terms, the language of binding and loosing means having the authority to interpret the Torah and apply it to particular situations. Those who have the power to "bind and loose" have the authority to establish rules for the community, to permit and forbid certain actions.

This authority was given by Christ to Peter, and it was then passed on to Peter's successors. The First Vatican Council recognized and defined what had been believed implicitly for over 1,800 years: the Bishop of Rome defines true doctrine without error when teaching about faith and morals as the Vicar of Christ. When we consider that no pope, at any time in history, has taught dogmatic error when acting in his official capacity as Pastor of the Universal Church, this belief becomes more understandable. As I mentioned earlier, during the fourth century nearly seventy percent of the world's bishops embraced some form of Arianism during its height. But it was the Bishop of Rome who upheld the true teachings of the Church, often nearly alone and always against tremendous opposition.

"Okay," your Fundamentalist friend replies, "but you're ignoring the fact that Peter denied Jesus three times. Obviously that isn't the sort of leader we're looking for." Yes, it is true that Peter denied the Lord three times. But this actually shows, in the end, that Peter's place was rock-solid. After His resurrection, Jesus appeared several times to His apostles, including one day on the shore of the Sea of Galilee (Jn 21). After they had finished breakfast, Jesus turns to Simon Peter and asks: "Simon, son of John, do you love me more than these?" (Jn 21:15). You can imagine what Peter is thinking: "Jesus is going to reprimand me because I denied Him three times the night of His arrest." Peter bravely prepares to face the music: "Yes, Lord; you know that I love you." And what does Jesus say? "Feed my lambs." He asks Peter the same question again and Peter again responds, probably with some astonishment: "Yes, Lord; you know that I love you." And Jesus said to him, "Tend my sheep." And then a third time: "Simon, son of John, do you love me?" Peter, we are told, was grieved and upset because Jesus asked him this question a third time. Was Jesus rubbing it in? Was He trying to make Peter look bad? Peter replies, "Lord, You know everything; you know that I love you." He is acknowledging that he knows that Jesus is well aware of his denials. And Jesus simply says, "Feed my sheep."

This often under-appreciated passage depicts Jesus and the apostles eating on the shores of the Sea of Galilee, the place where Jesus had fed the five thousand with loaves and fish, gave the Bread of Life discourse, and then emphatically stated five times that believers must eat His flesh and drink His blood. As He lovingly commands Peter to feed His lambs and tend His sheep, Jesus is purposefully calling to mind His teachings about the Bread of Life, the Eucharist. The three-fold repetition of Jesus' question is an emphatic reversal of Peter's three-fold denial (Jn 18:17, 25-27). Peter is still the rock; now he shall be the shepherd who feeds the flock of the Good Shepherd. He is to guide and tend the sheepfold, the Church of Jesus Christ. "There is one God and one Christ," wrote St. Cyprian, who lived in the third century, "and one Church, and one Chair founded on Peter by the word of the Lord. It is not possible to set up another altar or for there to be another priesthood besides that one altar and that one priesthood. Whoever has gathered elsewhere is scattering."

One Altar, One Body, One Church

The author of the epistle to the Hebrews speaks of that one altar, writing, "We have an altar, from which those who serve the tabernacle have no right to eat" (Heb 13:10). Who are the "we" that he refers to? A bit earlier he explains:

> But you have come to Mount Zion and to the city of the living God, the heavenly Jerusalem, and to myriads of angels, to the general assembly and church of the first-born who are enrolled

> in heaven, and to God, the Judge of all, and to the spirits of righteous men made perfect, and to Jesus, the mediator of a new covenant, and to the sprinkled blood, which speaks better than the blood of Abel. See to it that you do not refuse Him who is speaking (Heb 12:22-25).

The Church founded by Jesus upon Peter the Rock is the city of the living God and the heavenly Jerusalem. It is, Paul writes, the new Israel of God (Gal 6:16) and "the household of God, which is the church of the living God, the pillar and support of the truth" (1 Tm 3:15). It is the one, holy, catholic, and apostolic Church. It is the Church of the Good Shepherd, to which the Way leads, and in which the Truth is found and Life is given to the hungry and thirsty sheep.

Seeing that Jesus established a Church, that He gave authority to His apostles to guide that Church, and that those men passed on this authority to others, the question that must be asked and answered is: Where is that Church now? And what exactly is it? Is it merely an invisible union of all "true believers" as some fundamentalists and evangelicals believe? Is there more than one universal Church? Consider those questions in the light of the Old Testament, were there many Israels or just one? Was there one people of God or many? There are, Paul states, "many members, but one body" (1 Cor 12:20). The apostle to the Gentiles develops this more in his epistle to the Ephesians: "There is one body and one Spirit, just as also you were called in one hope of your calling; one Lord, one faith, one baptism, one God and Father of all who is over all and through all and in all" (Eph 4:4-6).

Paul's epistle to the Ephesians is filled with evidence of the Church's high place. The Church, as the Body of Christ, participates in Christ's authority: "And He put all things in subjection under His feet, and gave Him as head over all things to the church, which is His body, the fullness of Him who fills all in all" (Eph 1:22-23). The Church gives witness to the plan of God: ". . . in order that the manifold wisdom of God might now be made known through the church to the rulers and the authorities in the heavenly places" (Eph 3:10).

Paul continually refers to the Church as Christ's Body: "He is also head of the body, the church; and he is the beginning, the first-born from the dead; so that he himself might come to have first place in everything" (Col 1:18), and "Now I rejoice in my sufferings for your sake, and in my flesh I do my share on behalf of his body (which is the church) in filling up that which is lacking in Christ's afflictions" (Col 1:24). If the Church is Christ's Body, is it too much to suppose that it has some authority? And if the Church is Christ's Body, doesn't it make sense that the Church has both divine and human qualities? "The Church is both visible and spiritual," the *Catechism* states, "a hierarchical society and the Mystical Body of Christ. She is one, yet formed of two components, human and divine. That is her mystery, which only faith can accept" (CCC 779).

And if the Church is also the Bride of Christ, certainly she has immense value (see Eph 5:24-29). The Church is priceless, and of such value that she is the centerpiece of Christ's salvific work: "Husbands, love your wives, just as Christ also loved the church and gave himself up for her . . . that he might present to himself the church in all her glory, having no spot or wrinkle or any such thing; but that she should be holy and blameless" (Eph 5:25, 27).

Again, the authority of the Church resides in its head, Jesus Christ. He is the one who gives authority to the apostles as a whole and to Peter in a unique way: "And I tell you, you are Peter, and on this rock I will build my church, and the powers of death shall not prevail against it" (Mt 16:18; see Jn 21:15-19). Notice that the "powers of death" (in other translations, "the gates of hell") will not overcome the Church. If it were true, as many Christians apparently believe, that the Church fell into apostasy and can now be disregarded, then that would make our Lord a liar. Did many in the early Church fall away and pursue false teaching? Undoubtedly! Jesus Himself chose a man who would eventually betray him—Judas—as a disciple! If the Church is proven false or untrustworthy merely because people have left her, that proves too much, because then Jesus would be proven false and untrustworthy by the treacherous actions of Judas.

The question to ask is this: Did God establish a unified, universal Church (composed of local churches) with a visible structure of authority? Absolutely! In addition to Jesus' promise to Peter, we have His instructions regarding the discipline of wayward believers: "And if he refuses to listen to them, tell it to the church; and if he refuses to listen even to the church, let him be to you as a Gentile and a tax-gatherer" (Mt 18:17).

Many Fundamentalists insist the "true church" has no external structure or hierarchy. But the Acts of the Apostles consistently portray a Church with a structure of authority that is continued by ordaining new leaders by those already in leadership: "And when they had appointed elders for them in every church, having prayed with fasting, they commended them to the Lord in whom they had believed" (Acts 14:23). This was not merely a human work—it involved the guidance of the Holy Spirit: "Be on guard for yourselves and for all the flock, among which the Holy Spirit has made you overseers, to shepherd the church of God which He purchased with His own blood" (Acts 20:28). Paul teaches that it is God who has established the order of the Church and its ministry: "And God has appointed in the church, first apostles, second prophets, third teachers, then miracles, then gifts of healings, helps, administrations, various kinds of tongues" (1 Cor

12:28), all of which are meant for the good of the Church: "So also you, since you are zealous of spiritual gifts, seek to abound for the edification of the church" (1 Cor 14:12).

The Church has an altar. On that altar is the Eucharist, the Body and Blood of the Good Shepherd. In his encyclical, *Ecclesia de Eucharistia*, "On the Eucharist in Its Relationship to the Church," Pope John Paul II wrote these inspiring words:

> The Church draws her life from the Eucharist. This truth does not simply express a daily experience of faith, but recapitulates the heart of the mystery of the Church. In a variety of ways she joyfully experiences the constant fulfillment of the promise: "Lo, I am with you always, to the close of the age" (Mt 28:20), but in the Holy Eucharist, through the changing of bread and wine into the body and blood of the Lord, she rejoices in this presence with unique intensity. Ever since Pentecost, when the Church, the People of the New Covenant, began her pilgrim journey towards her heavenly homeland, the Divine Sacrament has continued to mark the passing of her days, filling them with confident hope (no. 1).

In the book of Revelation, Jesus says, "Behold, I stand at the door and knock; if anyone hears my voice and opens the door, I will come in to him, and will dine with him, and he with me" (Rv 3:20). The Good Shepherd wants to dine with us.

Chapter 7

The Body that Feeds the Body

As we saw in the previous chapter, the Bible shows us that the Church is the Body of Christ and that Peter has a central role. But what exactly is the role of the Church and Peter in the ongoing feeding of the faithful? In the sixth chapter of the gospel of John, we learn how Christians are to be fed and the role of the apostles in this effort. John 6 is a powerful passage of Scripture, perhaps the most important chapter in the New Testament with respect to spiritual food for Christians.

"But I don't feel any different after receiving the Eucharist," you might say. If that's the case, we need to dig deeper and look at our understanding of the Eucharist and at the beautiful explanation of the Mass and Eucharist given to us in John 6.

Go Tell (and Eat) It on the Mountain

In the next chapter we're going to look at the Passover context of John 6 in more detail. For now it is sufficient to point out that the Passover is an essential event in the gospel of John and in the evangelist's understanding of Jesus' life, death, and resurrection. The Passover is the ancient Jewish feast of unleavened bread, celebrating and commemorating the liberation of the Hebrews from Egypt (see Ex 12). John uses a specific phrase—"the Passover . . . was at hand"—three times in his gospel, one for each year of Jesus' ministry. And he uses it at the opening of this passage as a way of showing us how to pay attention to the context in which the events described take place: "Now the Passover, the feast of the Jews, was at hand" (Jn 6:4). The actions and words that follow point us toward the meaning of Jesus' ministry and explain how He is the Lamb of God, the one who will feed the sheep.

The four gospels, to varying degrees, make it clear that Jesus is the New Moses. He is the perfect prophet promised in Deuteronomy 18:18: "I will raise up a prophet from among their countrymen like you, and I will put my words in his mouth, and he shall speak to them all that I command him." The gospel writers make this connection with Moses clear. When they depict Jesus going up the mountain and delivering the Beatitudes, the guidelines and laws of the New Covenant (see Mt 5-7), they are drawing a parallel between Him and Moses, who ascended Mount Sinai to receive the Ten Commandments, the guidelines and laws of the Old Covenant (Ex 19ff). Of course, one big difference was that Moses, a great man but not divine, received those commandments from God, while Jesus, who is both God and man, delivers the new commandments by His own power, fulfilling the will of the Father.

John 6 also shows in another way that Jesus is the New Moses. "And Jesus went up on the mountain," we read, "and there He sat with His disciples" (v. 3). This is very similar to what happens prior to the Sermon on the Mount: "And when He saw the multitudes, He went up on the mountain; and after He sat down, His disciples came to Him" (Mt 5:1). But instead of giving the Sermon on the Mount, in which the spiritual and moral heart of the New Covenant was expressed and explained, Jesus demonstrates and explains the ritual meal of the New Covenant. Not only does He provide the people with more information about the nature of His Kingdom, He gives them profound insight into the nature of the King and how He provides nourishment for those in His Kingdom. Just as Moses went up the mountain and gave the people miraculous bread—*manna*—in the wilderness (Ex 16:4-21), Jesus goes up the mountain and gives the people miraculous bread. And He tells them of even more miraculous Bread—His very body and blood— that He will give them following His death and resurrection.

The significance of the feeding of the five thousand can be seen in the fact that it is the only miracle performed by Jesus (besides His resurrection) found in all four Gospels (Mt 15:29-39; Mk 6:34-44; Lk 9:12-17; Jn 6:1-14). Besides being an impressive demonstration of Jesus' power as the Son of God, it provides insight into the nature of the Mass and the structure of the Church.

The Sheep Without a Shepherd

In Mark's account, we read that Jesus "saw a great multitude, and he felt compassion for them because they were like sheep without a shepherd" (Mk 6:34). Jesus wants to care for His sheep. I cannot help but think of the many former Catholics who have come to me privately over the years with this huge dilemma: They don't know whom to trust. They have left the Church and now belong to some independent church. At first, life was great. But now they are having some problems with their pastor or the elders and don't know whom they can depend on. They aren't sure that Pastor Bill is teaching the truth. They don't know if their denomination is adhering to biblical teaching. They aren't convinced that they have a connection to the New Testament Church. But Jesus comes and says that He has compassion on them because they were like sheep without a shepherd. The Good Shepherd wants to bring them back home into the fullness of the sheepfold, the Catholic Church.

Jesus has compassion for the people who have gathered. But the disciples don't. They come up to Jesus and say, "The place is desolate and it is already quite late; send them away so that they may go into the surrounding countryside and villages and buy themselves something to eat" (Mk 6:35-36). The response of the disciples is the same one given to people by the world: "Are you hungry? Tough. Go away and fend for yourselves!" And what happens to those people? Some of them destroy their lives by feeding on drugs, pornography, or other destructive behaviors. Others deaden the hunger pains by becoming workaholics, building fortunes, or striving to be famous. Others look for food in New Age beliefs, Eastern mysticism, and "alternative" religions. But Jesus is waiting to feed them, if only they knew where to find Him. We must take them to the mountain and lead them to Jesus.

Jesus looks at the disciples and says, "*You* give them something to eat" (Mk 6:37; emphasis added). These are the men who are going to be priests and bishops. In other words, "You provide these lost and hungry sheep with food," the Good Shepherd tells them. What do they have? Nothing. They are helpless. "Where would we get so many loaves in a desolate place to satisfy such a great multitude?" (Mt 15:33). They are unable to feed the sheep on their own. They need Jesus; they rely on Him to provide the meal. And it's no different today. It is only through the power of the Holy Spirit that priests and bishops can consecrate bread and wine in celebrating the Eucharist. They, like all the faithful, rely on the Spirit and are dependent upon His compassion and mercy. What do the lay people have to give? A tiny loaf of faith and the words: "Lord, I am not worthy to receive you, but only say the words and I shall be healed."

This is the "great exchange" of the Mass, where we offer what we have, no matter how little it is, knowing that Jesus will take it and transform it. We offer our faith, along with bread and wine, and He gives us His Body, Blood, Soul, and Divinity. We give Him our words, and He gives us His Word.

The Model of the Mass

What do the disciples have to give the people? "We have five loaves and two fish," they say. Jesus responds, "That's enough, give them to me." He takes the meager pieces of bread and the small fish and says, "Have the people sit down" (Jn 6:10). They sit in the presence of the One who came to serve and not to be served.

"Jesus therefore took the loaves; and having given thanks, he distributed to those who were seated; likewise also of the fish as much as they wanted" (Jn 6:11). The sequence of actions is quite similar to what occurs at the Last Supper, when Jesus takes the bread, blesses it, breaks it, and gives it to His disciples—the same offering that takes place at the heart of the Mass.

Jesus is the one who performs the miracle, but how does He give the miraculous bread to the people? Through Peter and the disciples, with the guarantee of the Holy Spirit. "He took the seven loaves and the fish; and giving thanks, He broke them and started giving them to the disciples, and the disciples in turn, to the multitudes" (Mt 15:36; see also Mk 6:41; Lk 9:16). Interestingly, John doesn't mention this fact. He writes, "He distributed to those who were seated; likewise also of the fish as much as they wanted." Is there a contradiction? No, because the disciples, just like priests today, are acting on behalf of Christ. The *Catechism* teaches that "in the ecclesial service of the ordained minister, it is

Christ Himself who is present to His Church as Head of His Body, Shepherd of His flock, high priest of the redemptive sacrifice, Teacher of Truth. This is what the Church means by saying that the priest, by virtue of the sacrament of Holy Orders, acts *in persona Christi...*" (CCC 1548). St. Thomas Aquinas puts it this way: "Christ is the source of all priesthood: the priest of the old law was a figure of Christ, and the priest of the new law acts in the person of Christ."

Thus the disciples receive the commission to take the food of the Shepherd to the sheep. They are shepherds, with authority to watch over the flocks entrusted to them by the Chief Shepherd. Peter writes:

> So I exhort the elders among you, as a fellow elder and a witness of the sufferings of Christ as well as a partaker in the glory that is to be revealed. Tend the flock of God that is your charge, not by constraint but willingly, not for shameful gain but eagerly, not as domineering over those in your charge but being examples to the flock. And when the chief Shepherd is manifested you will obtain the unfading crown of glory. (1 Pt 5:1-4)

Catholic bishops are the successors of the apostles; they carry on the shepherding and feeding of Christ's flock—always by His power, authority, and grace. *Lumen Gentium*, the Second Vatican Council's Dogmatic Constitution on the Church, summarizes this important truth in this way: "Just as the office which the Lord confided to Peter alone, as first of the apostles, destined to be transmitted to his successors, is a permanent one, so also endures the office, which the apostles received, of shepherding the Church, a charge destined to be exercised without interruption by the sacred order of bishops" (par. 20; see CCC 862). Bishops and their co-workers, the priests, are "consecrated by the sacrament of Holy Orders, by which the Holy Spirit enables them to act in the person of Christ the head, for the service of all the members of the Church" (CCC 1142). Among the duties of the ordained "icon" of Christ is presiding at the Eucharist, in which bread and wine are changed into the Body and Blood of Jesus Christ. The prayer of the *Epiclesis* at Mass illustrates this dependence of the New Testament priesthood on the power of the Holy Spirit. "The *Epiclesis* ("invocation upon") is the intercession in which the priest begs the Father to send the Holy Spirit, the Sanctifier, so that the offerings may become the body and blood of Christ and [so] that the faithful, by receiving them, may themselves become a living offering to God" (CCC 1105).

Jesus feeds the people after He has been teaching them for many days (see Mk 6:34). This anticipates the two main parts of the Mass: the Liturgy of the Word and the Liturgy of the Eucharist. The people are fed in two ways, and Catholics today are also fed in two ways: by hearing the Word of God and by consuming the Incarnate Word of God. The first part of the Mass (or *Divine Liturgy*, as it is called in the Eastern Church) consists of a number of prayers and Scripture readings, along with a homily, the reciting of the Nicene Creed, and various greetings and responses. The fundamental patterns, prayers and elements of the Mass go back to the apostolic age and developed over the centuries. As the Acts of the Apostles indicates, the basic two-part pattern of the Mass was followed by early Christians in the first century: "And they were continually devoting themselves to the apostles' teaching and to fellowship, to the breaking of bread and to prayer" (Acts 2:42).

A few decades later, the same pattern is still in place. In the middle of the second century, Justin Martyr, wrote in his *First Apology*:

> And on the day called Sunday, all who live in cities or in the country gather together to one place, and the memoirs of the apostles or the writings of the prophets are read, as long as

> time permits; then, when the reader has ceased, the president verbally instructs, and exhorts to the imitation of these good things. Then we all rise together and pray, and, as we before said, when our prayer is ended, bread and wine and water are brought, and the president in like manner offers prayers and thanksgivings, according to his ability, and the people assent, saying Amen; and there is a distribution to each, and a participation of that over which thanks have been given, and to those who are absent a portion is sent by the deacons (par. 65-67; see CCC 1345).

Having left the Catholic Church in order to learn about the Bible and follow it more closely, I was amazed to see, upon studying the Mass and the liturgy of the Church, that the Mass almost in its entirety is based directly on Scripture. I was startled to discover that I was hearing more Scripture at Mass than was generally read in the Protestant churches I had attended. Now, after studying Church history, I see that I shouldn't have been too surprised. After all, the New Testament was written by members of the Church, was canonized by the authority of the Church, and was meant to be proclaimed publicly and interpreted from within the Church. In fact, the Bible could be called "The Catholic Book."

The first part of the Mass, called the *Liturgy of the Word*, consists of readings from the Old Testament, the Psalms, the New Testament epistles, and then the Gospel. The Gospel is always the high point of the Liturgy of the Word. Among the set prayers of the Mass are the Nicene Creed, which is filled with Scripture, and, of course, the Lord's Prayer. Furthermore, the Eucharistic prayers are loaded with Scripture and biblical images and themes, articulating salvation history and praising God for it. And at the heart of the Liturgy of the Eucharist are Christ's words, said by the priest, *in persona Christi*: "Take, eat, this is My Body, broken for you" and "Take, drink, this is the blood of the new and everlasting Covenant."

The two-part structure of the Mass is already evident in the feeding of the five thousand. After teaching the multitude, Jesus gives bread to the disciples, who in turn take the bread to the people. This has been the pattern of Eucharistic ritual and ceremony in the Church from the very beginning. Jesus, by the power of the Holy Spirit, offers His Body and Blood in the Eucharist to the people of God through the human instruments of the bishop and the priests. And when the people were fed and filled, Jesus said to the disciples "'Gather up the leftover fragments that nothing may be lost.' And so they gathered them up, and filled twelve baskets with fragments from the five barley loaves, which were left over by those who had eaten" (Jn 6:12-13). The special place granted by Jesus to the apostles is emphasized, as well as the abundant nature of the meal that He gives. It goes beyond anything that we could ever desire or dream about.

An important word is used twice in the story of the feeding of the five thousand—a word that does not appear anywhere else in the John's Gospel. It is the Greek verb *eucharisteo*, which means "to give thanks." It appears in verse 11—"Jesus therefore took the loaves; and *having given thanks*, He distributed to those who were seated"—and verse 23, which refers back to that moment: "There came other small boats from Tiberias near to the place where they ate the bread after the Lord *had given thanks*." Is it merely a coincidence that this all-important root word appears only these two times in the whole Gospel of John? Or that it is used twice in the same chapter Catholics understand to be referring to the Eucharist? Certainly not. The Eucharist is "an action of thanksgiving to God the *Father*" (CCC 1328), it is "the sacrificial memorial of *Christ* and his Body" and it is the presence of Christ "by the power of his word and of his Spirit" (CCC 1358).

There can be no doubt that the feeding of the five thousand shows that Jesus is able to provide bread for all and in abundance. This miracle foreshadows and represents the Eucharist, which Jesus will give through His Church to all who believe—everywhere and until the end of time.

The Ancient and Scriptural Structure of the Church

We have briefly described the role of bishops and priests in the Church and in the celebration of the Mass, but this issue bears closer inspection, because it is a stumbling block to many Protestants. This is especially so for those Fundamentalists and Evangelicals who believe an ordained priesthood is unbiblical and therefore contrary to God's will. Perhaps you have read or heard comments such as these: "The clerical Roman priesthood openly assaults the priesthood of all believers," or "'Clergyism' in all denominations is of the devil." These statements flow from the common Protestant argument that the Catholic priesthood was established many decades or even centuries after Christ. A certain Fundamentalist goes so far to say that "early Christianity was simple ... it did not have organization and was never meant to have it."

Scripture says otherwise. As we have seen, Jesus established Peter as the head of the apostles and gave him the keys to the Kingdom. In John's gospel Jesus breathes on the apostles and says to them, "Receive the Holy Spirit. If you forgive the sins of any, their sins are forgiven; if you retain the sins of any, they are retained" (Jn 20:22-23). If there were no structure to the Church, how could the apostles carry out their duties to bind and loose, to forgive sins, or to preside over their flock? How could they call together the local church and confront an unrepentant member (see Mt 18:15-18) if there is no leadership or authority?

In Acts 1, before the events of Pentecost, we find the disciples choosing someone to take the place of Judas. In verse 20 there is reference to the "office" of apostle and in verse 25 there is mention of the "ministry and apostleship" that Judas gave up by his betrayal. We find in the book of Acts numerous examples of the authority of the apostles, whether it be in preaching, distributing moneys, ministering to the poor or laying on of hands (imparting the Holy Spirit). Acts 15 records the first Church council as taking place in Jerusalem. A council, with apostles and elders in attendance, would seem to be clear evidence of some form of church organization. We also see that there is already a second generation of leaders in place, as evidenced by the authoritative speech of James (Acts 15:13-21), whom most scholars believe to be the author of the epistle of James.

I think that much of the confusion in this matter lies with the understanding of certain words relating to authority. While many non-Catholic Christians, particularly Evangelicals and Fundamentalists, dislike the use of the title "bishop," it is a faithful translation of the Greek word *episkopos*, which literally means "overseer." The title of *presbuteros* ("elder") is also interpreted as "bishop," although the word can also refer to "an old man" or "leader of families." There are several examples of this position of authority in the New Testament. In Acts 20, Paul, while at Ephesus, addresses the "elders of the church" (20:17) and urges them to "be on guard for yourselves and for all the flock, among which the Holy Spirit has made you overseers (*episkopous*), to shepherd the church of God, which He purchased with His own blood" (20:28). Such a remark could not have been made where there was no organization or structure of authority. (We also see that Paul again reveals his high regard for the

Church, which some Christians don't share). In Philippians 1:1, Paul and Timothy address the "overseers and deacons," and in 1 Timothy, Paul lists the requirements for the position of bishop (1 Tm 3:1-7). There are other places where the term is used as well (see Tit 1:5-9; 1 Pt 5:1-4).

So the early Church had numerous positions of authority and possessed an organized structure that included bishops. If we have any doubts on this point, we can look to the writings of the Church Fathers. Clement, who was the bishop of Rome in the years A.D. 92–101, wrote an epistle to the church at Corinth. After an extended discourse on the nature of the Christian life, Clement has this to say regarding the nature and origin of ecclesial (i.e., Church) order:

> The apostles received the gospel for us from Jesus Christ, and Jesus the Christ was sent from God. So Christ is from God, and the apostles are from Christ: thus both came in proper order by the will of God...So as [the apostles] preached from country to country and from city to city, they appointed their first converts, after testing them by the Spirit, to be the bishops and deacons of the future believers. Nor was this an innovation; since bishops and deacons had been written of long before... And is it any wonder, if those who in Christ were entrusted by God with such a duty should appoint those just mentioned? ...And our apostles knew through our Lord Jesus Christ that there would be strife over the title of bishop. So for this reason, because they had been given full foreknowledge, they appointed those mentioned above and afterward added the stipulation that if these should die, other approved men should succeed to their ministry (*1 Clement* 42-44).

Ignatius of Antioch (d. c. 110), seeking to ensure the unity of the Church, urged the Christians at Ephesus to follow their bishop:

> Therefore it is fitting for you to run your race together with the bishop's purpose—as you do. For your presbytery—worthy of

> fame, worthy of God—is attuned to the bishop like strings to a lyre. Therefore by your unity and harmonious love Jesus Christ is sung...Therefore it is profitable for you to be in blameless unison, so that you may always participate in God (1 Cor. 10:17). Let no one deceive himself: unless a man is within the sanctuary, he lacks the bread of God. If the prayer of one or two has such power (Mt 18:19-20), how much more does that of the bishop and the whole church? Therefore he who does not come to the assembly is already proud and has separated himself (*Letter to the Ephesians* 4-5).

According to Ignatius, the man who is outside the sanctuary lacks the bread of God. By God's grace, we have an invitation to eat at the altar and be fed by Our Lord. The Mass is our weekly, or even daily, opportunity to sit before the Good Shepherd, to hear His words, and to feast on Him. As we will now see in the second part of John 6, Jesus was entirely serious when He said He would feed us. But will we recognize and accept His shocking command to eat His flesh and drink His blood?

Chapter 8

Chew on This!

The people by the Sea of Tiberias have just been fed. They are satisfied—for now. Jesus directs the disciples to gather up the leftover scraps so that "nothing may be lost" (Jn 6:12). Once again, as when He fed the crowd, He works through His disciples; they do this work based on His command and authority. Note that this is the only miracle of Jesus in which the disciples are allowed to participate—a striking sign of the apostolic and episcopal authority that will be given to them as bishops in the early Church. But it is a curious command. After all, there has been plenty of food to eat already and everyone is satisfied. Why worry if some scraps are left for the wild animals? What was Jesus conveying to the apostles?

The answer lies in the connection between the twelve apostles and the twelve tribes of Israel, as well as in the unique place the apostles would have in the Church founded by Jesus. "The Lord Jesus endowed his community with a structure that will remain until the Kingdom is fully achieved," the *Catechism* explains, "Before all else there is the choice of the Twelve with Peter as their head. Representing the twelve tribes of Israel, they are the foundation stones of the New Jerusalem. The Twelve and the other disciples share in Christ's mission and his power, but also in his lot. By all his actions, Christ prepares and builds his Church" (CCC 765). Jesus had deliberately chosen twelve men to be the foundation of the new Israel, the Church. And although they were mortal, sinful men, they would share in His authority in astounding ways, including a special role on judgment day: "And Jesus said to them, 'Truly I say to you, that you who have followed Me, in the regeneration when the Son of Man will sit on His glorious throne, you also shall sit upon twelve thrones, judging the twelve tribes of Israel' " (Mt 19:28).

John writes, "And so they gathered them up, and filled twelve baskets with fragments from the five barley loaves, which were left over by those who had eaten" (Jn 6:13). Again, there is a foreshadowing of the Eucharist: the miraculous bread continues to be miraculous, even after all have been fed. It remains a gift from God, just as the Eucharist remains the true body and blood of Jesus after Mass. The twelve baskets represent the apostles' ongoing work of feeding the hungry and caring for their people. They also represent the abundance of God, the fullness they have received as God has poured out "grace upon grace" upon them (Jn 1:16).

This superabundance of food—first natural food and then later supernatural food—is captured in Jesus' statement, "I am the bread of life; he who comes to me shall not hunger, and he who believes in me shall never thirst" (Jn 6:35). Those who are hungry for Jesus will come to him—through the apostles and His Church. There is also a contrast with another sort of miraculous food, the manna of the Old Testament. Once they were filled with the manna and their appetite was satisfied for a while, the people would have no more. "Morning by morning they gathered it," we read, "each as much as he could eat; but when the sun grew hot, it melted" (Ex 16:21). There was a limit. But there is no limit when it comes to the provision offered by Jesus; it overflows and goes beyond our wildest dreams. In the New Covenant, we never hunger—unless we choose not to eat the Bread of Life.

The Passover Connection

In order to appreciate what follows in the latter part of the sixth chapter of John's Gospel, we need to look at the larger context of the passage. Of primary importance is the Passover, the great Jewish feast of unleavened bread celebrating the salvation of the Hebrews from the land of Egypt (see Ex 12). John focuses on this feast in particular, and he specifically uses a phrase highlighting this fact—"the Passover ... was at hand"—three times in his Gospel, one for each year of Jesus' ministry. It's as though he were waving his arms and saying, "Hey! Check this out! I've got an important connection to make." And he sure does, for in each of the three places where the Passover is mentioned, it is explicitly related to Jesus' death and resurrection.

The second chapter of John's Gospel depicts Jesus in Jerusalem during the Passover (2:13). In this first Passover, Jesus cleanses the Temple and then prophecies, rather cryptically, His death and resurrection:

> Jesus answered them, "Destroy this temple, and in three days I will raise it up." The Jews then said, "It has taken forty-six years to build this temple, and will you raise it up in three days?" But he spoke of the temple of his body.
> (Jn 2:19-21)

In the sixth chapter we read about the second Passover during Jesus' public ministry. Eventually in His long discourse Jesus teaches again about His death and resurrection (Jn 6:51); we will examine this in more detail later. And the third Passover, of course, is when Jesus is arrested, tried, and crucified (see Jn 19:14).

The Passover context is significant for a number of reasons. At the heart of this Jewish feast was a solemn ceremony in remembrance of the Exodus from Egypt, a most pivotal and defining moment in Jewish history. At that first Passover the people were commanded to take an unblemished lamb (Ex 12:3–27), kill it, and spread the blood over their door posts and lintels (v. 7). And then they were commanded to eat the lamb completely (vs. 8–10). In addition to the lamb, the people were to eat unleavened bread (v. 15). So down through history, until the time of Jesus, the Jews had celebrated the Passover with a feast involving bread and wine and the singing of certain Psalms, followed by the sacrificing of lambs in the Temple.

It is not accidental that John, in describing the beginning of Jesus' ministry, describes Him as the "Lamb of God" (Jn 1:29, 36). Nor are Jesus' words regarding the Temple unrelated, just as it isn't mere trivia that Jesus was condemned to die at the sixth hour (Jn 19:14). That was the time of day—between noon and 3:00 p.m.—when the slaughtering of the lambs for Passover began in the Temple. There are clues in the details as well. For instance, John notes more than once that the legs of Jesus were not broken (Jn 19:33, 36). Why? Because He was the perfect Passover Lamb, without blemish or broken bones, just as the Pentateuch required: "They shall leave none of it [the Passover lamb] until morning, nor break a bone of it; according to all the statute of the Passover they shall observe it" (Num 9:12). John plainly believes there is a significant relationship between Jesus and the Passover, and that relationship involves the Eucharist and John 6. Although John's Gospel does not have a Last Supper narrative, there are many elements in it which tie the words of Jesus in John 6 to the Last Supper.

John's Apocalypse, the book of Revelation, also presents Jesus as the true Lamb, the fulfillment of the Passover sacrifices. Jesus is vividly described as "a Lamb standing, as if slain..." (Rv 5:6). This is not unique to just John. Paul writes in his first epistle to the Corinthians that "Christ our Passover also has been sacrificed. Let us therefore sacrifice the feast..." (1 Cor 5:7-8). Later, Paul compares three altars: those of the pagans, the Jews, and the Christians (1 Cor 10:14ff). He asks, "Is not the cup of blessing which we bless a sharing in the blood of Christ? Is not the bread which we break a sharing in the body of Christ? ...for we all partake of the one bread" (vs. 16-17). This parallels, in a striking manner, Christ's words in John 6: "I am the bread of life. . . .He who eats my flesh and drinks my blood abides in me, and I in him" (Jn 6:48, 56). All of these point to the same astonishing truth: The Passover Lamb is offered to us as divine food—life-giving flesh and blood.

The *Catechism of the Catholic Church* teaches that "in the Old Covenant bread and wine were offered in sacrifice among the first fruits of the earth as a sign of grateful acknowledgment to the Creator. But they also received a new significance in the context of the Exodus: the unleavened bread that Israel eats every year at Passover commemorates the haste of the departure that liberated them from Egypt; the remembrance of the manna in the desert will always recall to Israel that it lives by the bread of the Word of God; their daily bread is the fruit of the promised land, the pledge of God's faithfulness to His promises." It then states that the "cup of blessing," the third cup in the Jewish Passover meal, "adds to the festive joy of wine an eschatological dimension: the messianic expectation of the rebuilding of Jerusalem. When Jesus instituted the Eucharist, he gave a new and definitive meaning to the blessing of the bread and the cup" (CCC 1334). Let's take a look at how, in John 6, Jesus conveyed the astonishing truth about the Eucharist.

Can You Feel the Tension Building?

Any good interpretation of John 6 must note the purposeful and pointed escalation of tension between Jesus and the Jews. This is a four-part progression, with each of the parts marked by Jesus saying "Truly, truly" (or "Amen, amen"). This was a Semitic manner of signifying a teaching of great importance (vs. 26, 32, 47, and 53), but also of connecting concepts together, forming a bridge between what had already been said and what was about to be revealed. So throughout John 6 there is a logical progression and a series of connections that Jesus wants to make clear, a transition from the temporal and natural to the eternal and supernatural.

The first part begins when the people ask him, upon His arrival, "Rabbi, when did you get here?" (v. 25). He points out that all they desire is a free meal (v. 25-27). "Jesus answered them and said, 'Truly, truly, I say to you, you seek me, not because you saw signs, but because you ate of the loaves, and were filled.'" (v. 26). He rebukes them for seeking only earthly, temporal food and tells them they must believe in Him (v. 29). This is Jesus' call for them to believe that He was sent by God.

The second part begins with the people asking for sign so that they might believe He is of God (v. 30-31, 34). Never mind that just a while before they had declared, "This is indeed the prophet who is to come into the world" (v. 14)! Having witnessed Jesus miraculously providing food, they then refer to the manna, the miraculous food given by God to the Hebrews during their forty years of wandering in the desert. They are trying to egg Him on, hoping for another free meal. "Jesus therefore said to them, 'Truly, truly, I say to you, it was not Moses who gave you the bread from heaven; my Father gives you the true bread from heaven'" (Jn 6:32). He then demands another step of faith: "For this is the will of my Father, that every one who sees the Son and believes in him should have eternal life; and I will raise him up at the last day" (v. 40). This is Jesus' call to believe that He is the Messiah and Savior.

The third part of this progression begins with the people grumbling (v. 41) and wondering how a mere mortal could claim that He had come down from heaven (v. 42). Jesus tells them to stop grumbling and emphatically states that belief in Him *is* eternal life: "Truly, truly, I say to you, he who believes has eternal life. I am the bread of life. (Jn 6:47-8). While the Jews refer to Jesus as the "son of Joseph" (v. 42), Jesus identifies Himself as the Son of the Heavenly Father (v. 46). This is Jesus' call to believe that He is the Son of God and the Bread of Life.

So far, so good. We sense that the Jews are getting agitated, but the situation is still under control. People are mildly perturbed, but nobody is too upset. At this point the people and Jesus are just engaging in a lively debate about theological issues. But that changes as Jesus moves on to His final and most astounding point: "I am the living bread which came down from heaven; if any one eats of this bread, he will live for ever; *and the bread which I shall give for the life of the world is my flesh*" (v. 51, emphasis added). No longer is the bread just a symbol (the Bread of Life) or a sign (the manna); it is now a sacrament—a sign that becomes what it signifies. Jesus' Body doesn't merely *represent* the Bread of Life; it *is* the Bread of Life.

This stunning revelation is marked by the fourth and final "Amen, Amen," indicating that this is the final and greatest of Jesus' declarations on the matter. "Truly, truly, I say to you," He states, "unless you eat the flesh of the Son of Man and drink His blood, you have no life in you" (Jn 6:53). In case there is any doubt about the meaning of His astounding statement, Jesus repeats it—not once, or twice, or even three times, but *four* times in the next four verses:

> He who eats my flesh and drinks my blood has eternal life, and I will raise him up at the last day. For my flesh is food indeed, and my blood is drink indeed. He who eats my flesh and drinks my blood abides in me, and I in him. As the living Father sent me, and I live because of the Father, so he who eats me will live because of me (Jn 6:54-7).

This is stunning, shocking language. We can only imagine the silent astonishment of those listening to him. Who does this carpenter think he is? What kind of madness is he proclaiming? Those listening knew that the eating and drinking of blood of animals— let alone humans—was specifically forbidden in the Pentateuch: "Only be sure that you do not eat the blood; for the blood is the life, and you shall not eat the life with the flesh" (Dt 12:23). And cannibalism was a sure sign of God's judgment, the result of a curse (see Lv 26:27-29; Ez 5:10).

This, then, raises the question: "Is eating the body of Christ cannibalism?" And "why would we be able to drink the blood of Christ and not the blood of animals?" The Scriptures are clear that life is in the blood, and that drinking the blood of the animal represents an identification with the life of the animal. Man is not permitted to drink the blood of animals because man is not created in the image of an animal, rather in the image of God. Therefore, there is only one cup of blood that would be permitted for man to drink—the blood of God—because we are created in the image of God. Strictly speaking, cannibalism is the eating of dead human flesh. The body of Christ that we consume is living, not dead.

Note that Jesus does not explain away His words as a metaphor or hyperbole. When He sees their astonishment, He doesn't hasten to say, "Wait, I was just speaking symbolically about accepting me as your personal Lord and Savior." He doesn't calm them by explaining, "I was just using a metaphor to take advantage of this wonderful teaching moment." No, He repeats His statement, asserting that His flesh "is the bread which came down from heaven, not such as the fathers ate and died; he who eats this bread will live for ever" (Jn 6:58).

This is Jesus' call to believe in the Eucharist. It is the call to come to the altar and to feed on the flesh and blood of the final and perfect Passover Lamb, to eat and be fully satisfied, to consume and be transformed. "Is not the cup of blessing which we bless a sharing in the blood of Christ?" asks Paul. "Is not the bread which we break a sharing in the body of Christ?" (1 Cor 10:16). Yes, it most certainly is, praise God! Jesus gives Himself to us so that we might become intimately joined to Him: "Since there is one bread, we who are many are one body; for we all partake of the one bread" (1 Cor 10:17). He wants to feed us. Do we want to be fed?

The Incarnational Logic of the Eucharist

After a spectacular moment in a sporting event, a television broadcast will almost always show a replay. The sportscasters will look at the jump shot from a new angle, they'll show the grand slam in slow motion, or they'll freeze the shot of the spectacular touchdown catch in the end zone. We have just been listening to one of the most spectacular discourses in the Bible, the sort of passage that we can return to every day of our life and never tire of studying and pondering.

Let's revisit John 6 and pay special attention to the development of the "Incarnational logic" in Jesus' actions and teachings. By this we mean the way in which Jesus bases His astonishing doctrine about the Eucharist on the fact that He is the Incarnate Word, the God-man. All Christians, whether Protestant, Catholic, or Orthodox, agree that Jesus is God. Along with the Trinity, the divinity of Christ is the most central belief of the Christian faith: "By this you know the Spirit of God: every spirit which confesses that Jesus Christ has come in the flesh is of God" (1 Jn 4:2; see CCC 463). Christians have a common understanding of John's statement in the opening chapter of his Gospel that "the Word became flesh, and dwelt among us, and we beheld His glory, glory as of the only begotten from the Father, full of grace and truth" (Jn 1:14). Yet, as we saw earlier, there are very different understandings of what Jesus means in John 6. One reason for this is that many Christians do not follow the Incarnational principle through to its logical conclusion.

Jesus couldn't begin His public ministry by announcing to the crowds that He is God-Incarnate and that He was going to give them His flesh to eat and His blood to drink. He had to spend many months and countless hours teaching His apostles, then preaching among the people in the synagogues, the wilderness, and the villages. He healed the sick and the lame and He declared that the Kingdom was at hand.

At the time described in John 6, Jesus had been ministering for about two years. On that day "Jesus went away to the other side of the Sea of Galilee" (Jn 6:1). Earlier, in John 5, He had healed a crippled man at the pool of Bethesda (Jn 5:1-15), demonstrating that He had been sent from God. Those Jews who were seeking to quiet Him clearly recognized that He was making bold and unique claims. "For this cause therefore the Jews were seeking all the more to kill Him," John writes, "because He not only was breaking the Sabbath, but also was calling God His own Father, making Himself equal with God" (Jn 5:18). The remainder of John 5 is a lengthy explanation by Jesus of His relationship with the Father and the reasons He had been sent into the world. All of this points to Jesus' divinity, even if it isn't always openly stated.

So Jesus has been healing and teaching. But the people need more. Healings are wonderful and teaching is important, but they aren't enough. The people need Him. They need a life-changing encounter with Jesus that is more than seeing or hearing, as necessary and good as those acts are. Jesus, seeing a great multitude coming to Him (Jn. 6:5), decides to feed them: physically and spiritually. Both actions require supernatural power, and both go beyond what the people would naturally expect.

First, as we have seen, He physically feeds the five thousand with ordinary physical bread (6:11, 26) provided by extraordinary means. In this manner His power and divine nature are revealed, at least to those who are willing to look deeper than their next meal. The people understand that He is not an ordinary man, but that He is the Prophet sent into the world (Jn 6:14).

Secondly, Jesus states that He is "the bread of life" (6:48) and that belief in Him is necessary for eternal life (6:50). Here He calls the people to trust in Him as God and to accept and confess that He is divine and the source of eternal life. He is a Prophet, but He is also the greatest and perfect Prophet—the one who fulfills what He professes and prophesies. All Christians agree that this is so because they agree that Jesus is God-Incarnate, sent by the Father to save the world (see Jn 3:16).

The disagreements among Christians about this passage and the Eucharist start with Jesus' final "Amen, Amen," (Jn 6:53) and His unwavering insistence that His "flesh" is the bread of life (v. 51). He further teaches that His flesh "is true food" and tells the people that they must eat of His flesh in order to enter into a life-giving, eternal relationship with Him. As we'll see in more detail in the next chapter, this is also where disagreements arise between Jesus and His disciples, not just between Him and the Jewish leaders:

> Many therefore of His disciples, when they heard this said, "This is a difficult statement; who can listen to it?" But Jesus, conscious that His disciples grumbled at this, said to them, "Does this cause you to stumble? (vs. 60-1)

What *has* caused them to stumble? Is it Jesus' claim that He is the unique Son of God? Is it His growing insistence that He is God—an insistence that culminates in His declaration in John 8, "Truly, truly, I say to you, before Abraham was born, I am" (Jn 8:58). Is it His claim that it is faith in Him that brings salvation?

No, it is not. Here is where, I am convinced, having taught it for many years as a Protestant pastor, the deficiencies of a metaphorical interpretation of Christ's words become evident. Interpreting Jesus' command to eat His flesh and drink His blood as a metaphor for a "personal relationship" or "accepting Him as Lord and Savior" is not enough. It does not correspond to the intention of Jesus' words, nor do justice to His role as the Passover Lamb. Yes, it is true that eating His flesh and drinking His blood in Holy Communion are part of a deep relationship with the Person of Jesus. What other relationship could it provide? And it is a fact that receiving Eucharist is an acceptance into our bodies of our Lord and Savior. But it is not merely a metaphor, or simply a symbol, or just a pleasant sentiment.

The logic is plain to see: Jesus feeds the people literal bread. He offers literal eternal life to those who literally believe in him. He uses the metaphor of the Bread of Life, but does so to connect the reality of His feeding of the five thousand to the reality of His miraculous feeding of those who believe in Him. Just as He is able miraculously to provide natural bread to feed the body, so too He will miraculously provide the supernatural bread—His flesh—to feed the spirit. How will this be done? By means of a sacrament, which is a concrete, logical, and supernatural continuation of the Incarnation.

Unfortunately, some people (including many Catholics) think the sacraments are mere human inventions, or some form of Christianized magic, or just empty works. The *Catechism* corrects these misunderstandings by providing a concise, two-part definition of a sacrament. First, "The sacraments are perceptible signs (words and actions) accessible to our human nature" (CCC 1084a). The sacraments aren't abstract notions or empty words, but are signs—water, oil, wine, and bread—that are concrete and material in nature. We can see, feel, and taste them. Secondly, "By the action of Christ and the power of the Holy Spirit they make present efficaciously the grace that they signify" (CCC 1084b). So baptism, by the work of Jesus Christ and the power of the Holy Spirit, does not just symbolize the washing away of sins, but actually does wash away sins. Peter writes that "baptism now saves you—not the removal of dirt from the flesh, but an appeal to God for a good conscience—through the resurrection of Jesus Christ . . ." (1 Pt 3:21). The Eucharist does not just symbolize the flesh and blood of Jesus Christ, but *is* that very flesh and blood, truly offered now in an unbloody, miraculous, and sacramental manner.

The *Catechism* also explains that "the sacraments are efficacious signs of grace, instituted by Christ and entrusted to the Church, by which divine life is dispensed to us" (CCC 1131). Because they are the work of Jesus and not simply human creations, the sacraments convey His life to us and make us "partakers of the divine nature" (2 Pt 1:4). The sacraments impart spiritual power and grace because they flow from the Second Person of the Trinity, who became flesh and blood and entered time and space in order to bring salvation and spiritual life.

Simply put, we know that material things can convey spiritual power because God became man in order to save us! Because Jesus is the New Adam and desires to have close communion with those who are new creatures, He uses His Body as the means by which we are transformed and become more like Him: "Take, eat; this is My body" (Mt 26:26). Incorporated sacramentally into Christ, we not only receive Christ—He receives each of us. In the words of Pope John Paul II, in his beautiful encyclical on the Eucharist, *Ecclesia*

De Eucharistia: "He enters into friendship with us: 'You are my friends' (Jn 15:14). Indeed, it is because of him that we have life: 'He who eats me will live because of me' (Jn 6:57). Eucharistic communion brings about in a sublime way the mutual 'abiding' of Christ and each of his followers: 'Abide in me, and I in you' (Jn 15:4)" (par. 22).

Nourishment for Life Everlasting

Let's look at the sacraments and the Eucharist from a slightly different perspective. On the natural plane, we enter into this world through physical birth. We are fed physical food, our minds are educated and developed, and our emotions mature and grow as well. In an analogous but completely real way the sacraments give us birth, nourish us, and pour God's life into us. We enter into the family of God through a new birth, the sacrament of baptism. Baptism frees us from sin and by it we are reborn as sons of God. (CCC 1213; see Rom 6:4; 1 Pt 3:21). At baptism, we are filled with sanctifying grace, which is the very life of God, and made "'a new creature,' an adopted son of God, who has become a 'partaker of the divine nature . . .'" (CCC 1265). This is how we enter the Church and become members of the Body of Christ (CCC 1267). As in the natural realm, we can only be born into this new life one time, for baptism leaves an eternal, "indelible spiritual mark of [our] belonging to Christ" (CCC 1272).

God loves us, and as our Father, He wants to provide His family, the Church, with the best food and nourishment. The greatest meal He provides is Holy Communion, for the Eucharist is Jesus Himself and is "the source and summit of the Christian life" (CCC 1324). What could be more astonishing and humbling than receiving the very Body, Blood, Soul, and Divinity of the God-man into your own body? By uniting Himself to humanity, the Son becomes, in the Eucharist, the source of unity for the entire family of God, "the sublime cause of that communion in the divine life and that unity of the People of God by which the Church is kept in being" (CCC 1325).

The Eucharist, as Bishop Fabian Bruskewitz has said, is the "great exchange": God gives Himself to us, and we give ourselves back in return. It is the offering of ourselves as sons and daughters of God and as members of Christ's Body to the Father. It is the sacrifice of Christ made really and truly present (CCC 1362-1367). As Christ's Body we offer ourselves in union with Him as sacrifice and intercession (CCC 1368). In the Eucharist we experience unity with one another and "an intimate union with Christ Jesus" (1391).

All of this amazing and heady theology points to a single, simple goal: communion with God. That supernatural communion is both the focus of the sacramental life *and* the source of divine life. Each of the sacraments is oriented in a specific and complementary way toward our salvation and the final goal of heaven. Through and by the sacraments we are conformed to Christ. The Holy Spirit—the "Spirit of adoption"—makes the Catholic faithful "partakers in the divine nature by uniting them in a living union with the only Son, the Savior" (CCC 1129).

Through the sacraments we are truly made children of God (see 1 Jn 3:1-10) and partakers of the divine nature (CCC 1692; 2 Pt 1:4) and now "participate in the life of the Risen Lord" (CCC 1694). This means that Christ is the center and focus of our lives—at least He should be! He is, the *Catechism* declares, "the first and last point of reference" for all things (CCC 1698). He is the reason for living; He has given us everything that we have and is making us everything that we will be. Our lives are to be conformed and patterned to His life, the life of a Son. We are divine sons who follow the One Son: "He who believes in Christ becomes a son of God. This filial adoption transforms him by giving him the ability to follow the example of Christ" (CCC 1709).

Remember Abraham? He was about to sacrifice Isaac. God had entered into a covenant with him that would bring blessings to the entire world. Yet there Abraham was, ready to sacrifice the son who was the personification of that blessing—if he died, the blessing also died. And the little boy said to his father, his eyes wide and innocent, "Abba (Daddy), I've got the wood and I've got the fire, but where is the sacrifice?" And Abraham, in anguish, simply said, "God will provide." Then he tied up Isaac, took his knife, and prepared himself for what he had to do. You know what happened next. All of a sudden, Abraham stopped, hearing a ram in the thicket. "God will provide the lamb." Isaac was saved, but the expectation of God's lamb continued.

Now, fast forward two thousand years. John the Baptist is out in the desert preaching and baptizing. He is spending his life trying to reach the people of Israel, but he knows that his personal sacrifice isn't enough. He expects something more, since he is just the messenger. He is not the Messiah, but he is preparing the way for Him. "God will provide," John thinks, faithful to his calling. And then, one momentous day, God does provide. John looks up and sees Jesus approaching. He recognizes the supernatural provision of God—the same God who gave manna to the Hebrews in the desert centuries before—and he declares: "Behold the Lamb of God who takes away the sins of the world."

Jesus is the Lamb sent to be sacrificed on our behalf, for our lives, and for our sins. "For Christ our Passover also has been sacrificed," Paul exclaims, "Let us therefore celebrate the feast" (1 Cor 5:7-8). Jesus declares: "He who eats my flesh and drinks my blood has eternal life" (Jn 6:54). The heavenly feast has been prepared, the banquet table is set, and it's time to be fed. Will we accept the invitation to eat the flesh and drink the blood of the Lamb?

Chapter 9

True Food for Malnourished Faith

The table is set and Jesus is offering His Body and Blood to us. But many refuse the offer. And they aren't just non-Christians. I know this from sad, personal experience.

While being raised in the Catholic Church, I received the Eucharist every week. I took Jesus Christ into my body each time I received Holy Communion—but I didn't understand what I was doing and whom I was receiving. And after leaving the Catholic Church and becoming a Protestant pastor, I denounced the Catholic belief in the Real Presence as illogical, unbiblical, superstitious, unnecessary, and even disgusting. How, I argued, could anyone believe that Jesus' words in John 6 had anything to do with the Eucharist? How could people believe that Jesus' command to eat His flesh and drink His blood must be taken literally? It was outrageous and appalling. It was difficult—and I didn't want that difficulty in my life. I was happy and I loved my congregation. I was being fed by reading the Bible, praying, and experiencing wonderful friendships and fellowship.

This *is* a Difficult Statement!

I cannot count the number of times I read John 6 in my twelve years as a Protestant. I knew it inside and out, or so I thought. But when I began to sense that something was lacking and I started to study Catholic doctrine, I finally saw what I had missed. There was food on the table, and I had ignored it. I now understood that the difficulty I had with the Catholic teaching about John 6 and the Eucharist was really a difficulty with Jesus Himself.

As I read John 6 again, I could hear Jesus asking me: "Does this cause you to stumble?" (v. 61). Yes, Lord, I thought to myself, it does. But I want to believe. I want to understand. And so, in order to understand I had to grapple with all of the arguments I had used against the belief in the Real Presence. These are the same arguments that many Fundamentalists, Evangelicals, Pentecostal, and sometimes even mainline Protestants use in trying to refute the belief that the Catholic Church, along with the Orthodox Churches, has held for two thousand years. Let's take a look at those arguments and the Catholic responses to them, seeking to understand better the astonishing love and gifts of God.

Is it any wonder that many of Jesus' disciples, when they heard His shocking words, said, "This is a difficult statement; who can listen to it?" (v. 60)? Even after spending so much time with the Bread of Life, they are not able to accept all of His teachings. And Jesus knew it. He recognized all along that some of the disciples were lacking in faith, had impure motives, or were pursuing a different agenda. So He states, "But there are some of you who do not believe" (v. 64). He reads their hearts and knows their weakness. Of course, seeing this breaks His heart. As the Good Shepherd, He doesn't want to lose even one sheep. But He will not water down the Truth, as startling and demanding as it is. And so, John tells us, "As a result of this many of His disciples withdrew, and were not walking with Him anymore" (v. 66).

This marks the only time in the Gospels that disciples leave Jesus over a doctrinal matter. The sheep leave the

Shepherd and go without the true food of the Eucharist. Every time I read these verses, I remember that I left the Catholic Church because I thought I wasn't being fed. And yet Jesus was saying, "He who eats my Flesh and drinks my Blood abides in me and I in him." He declared, "My Flesh is true food." Yet I imagined that I wasn't getting the right spiritual diet. I thought that I was starving on the Catholic meal plan and that the Assemblies of God had the ultimate food and most satisfying spiritual spreads.

The Ascension is the Heavenly Ticket

I was puzzled, however, by the statement Jesus made after pointing out that the disciples are stumbling. He said, "What then if you should behold the Son of Man ascending where He was before?" (Jn 6:62). Why does He talk about ascending? What does that have to do with eating His flesh and drinking His blood?

The answer can be found a little earlier, when the first grumbling starts among the people. They were bothered that Jesus had declared, "I am the bread that came down out of heaven" (v. 41), and they asked, "How does He now say, 'I have come down out of heaven'?" (Jn 6:42). They understood that Jesus was no longer claiming to merely be a prophet or great teacher—He was making a bold declaration of a unique relationship with God the Father. He had done the same thing earlier in John's Gospel, saying, "And no one has ascended into heaven, but He who descended from heaven, even the Son of Man" (Jn 3:13; see 20:17). In bringing up the Ascension in the context of His teaching about the Eucharist, Jesus is stressing the literal nature of His words, for He would literally ascend into heaven (Acts 1:9-10), just as He had literally come down from heaven (Jn 1:14). This is another one of those sayings that would later "come true" for the disciples, causing them suddenly to exclaim "Ah-ha!" at the proper moment down the road. The evangelist himself describes this "time-release" learning in the second chapter of his Gospel: "When therefore He was raised from the dead, His disciples remembered that He said this; and they believed the Scripture, and the word which Jesus had spoken" (Jn 2:22).

Jesus is also making the point that, since He has a unique relationship with the Father and is in fact God, what is there to keep Him from offering us His flesh and blood? Is it reasonable to accept the truth that Jesus is the Incarnate Word, the Second Person of the Trinity, but then to doubt that He can offer His body and blood to us in some new and mysterious manner? Which is more amazing: that the infinite God would become a finite man, or that once He was a finite man He would offer Himself to us under the appearance of finite bread and wine? Once again, we see the Incarnational logic.

Furthermore this reference to the Ascension helps the disciples to understand in what manner Jesus' body can be offered to them: It is a glorified, resurrected body. No other kind of body can ascend into heaven—a natural body can be *assumed* into heaven, but cannot *ascend* into heaven. This indicates that the Eucharist is the true Body and Blood of Jesus, but in a supernatural, sacramental manner—not a natural manner. "The sacrifice of Christ and the sacrifice of the Eucharist are *one single sacrifice*," the *Catechism of the Catholic Church* teaches, yet "the manner of offering is different" being unbloody but still "truly propitiatory" —that is, able to atone for our sins (CCC 1367). The fact that Jesus entered the upper room through locked doors on Easter night and ascended into heaven forty days later in plain view of His disciples demonstrated that His risen Body was transformed and that it now exists in a spiritual mode. The Eucharist is

Jesus' true flesh and blood, but offered in a supernatural way, beyond the comprehension of human intellect. The manner of His presence under the appearances of bread and wine is unique (see CCC 1374). It takes faith to believe that God became man. And it takes faith to believe that Jesus rose from the dead and ascended into heaven. Similarly, it takes faith to believe that "in the most blessed sacrament of the Eucharist 'the body and blood, together with the soul and divinity, of our Lord Jesus Christ and, therefore, the whole Christ is *truly, really, and substantially* contained'" (CCC 1374).

The Spirit and the Flesh

Very well, you may say, but what about the next sentence in the Gospel discourse: "It is the Spirit who gives life; the flesh profits nothing; the words that I have spoken to you are spirit and are life" (Jn 6:63)? This is a favorite verse for many Fundamentalists, who claim that it conclusively destroys the Catholic interpretation of all that went before it.

The reason for this Fundamentalist position is their belief that a physical object or act cannot achieve an inward effect and change. Former Catholic and now Fundamentalist apologist James G. McCarthy readily admits this in his book *The Gospel According to Rome* (Harvest House, 1995). Writing about Jesus' words in John 6:51-57, McCarthy argues that "eternal life was to be obtained by believing Jesus' words. Eating his flesh would be profitless" (p. 142). After declaring that the Catholic belief in the Eucharist is idolatrous and that the worship of objects is a grave sin, McCarthy writes, "We can be sure that God will never contradict Himself by entering into material objects such as bread and wine and then ordering people to worship them" (p. 143).

If that's the case, both Catholics *and* Fundamentalists have a serious problem, because God did enter into the material realm and He did take on flesh: "And the Word became flesh, and dwelt among us" (Jn 1:14). As Paul tells the Colossians, in Jesus "all the fullness of Deity dwells in bodily form" (Col 2:9). In other words, the promise of God—regeneration and spiritual empowerment—was realized and actualized in the outward, physical manifestation of grace: Jesus Christ! As the *Catechism* explains, "The saving work of [Christ's] holy and sanctifying humanity is the sacrament of salvation, which is revealed and active in the Church's sacraments" (CCC 774). McCarthy, unwittingly, proves far too much by his argument, and because of his blind dislike for the Catholic Church, essentially does away with the Incarnation.

I can appreciate his confusion, because I once shared it. I finally saw, thank heavens, that this approach to denying the Eucharist contains dangerous neo-Gnostic and rationalistic tendencies. This is evident in McCarthy's insistence that the Catholic belief in the Real Presence must be false because "there is not even the slightest indication that either the bread or the wine changed at the Last Supper." He adds that the same is true at Mass. "The bread and wine before and after the consecration look exactly alike. Furthermore, they smell, taste, and feel the same. In fact, all empirical evidence supports the interpretation that they do not change at all" (p. 133).

This reliance on "empirical evidence" raises questions that most Fundamentalists avoid or don't even consider. Since when does Christianity rest on scientific evidence? Where is the empirical evidence for the Virgin Birth? Or for the existence of angels? Or of the Holy Spirit? What about heaven—does anyone have photos? And where is the laboratory-tested proof that Jesus was completely man *and* completely God? If Jesus had given a tissue sample on the shores of Galilee, would His DNA have registered as the

DNA of God? Or would it look like ordinary human DNA? Didn't the people say, "Is not this Jesus, the son of Joseph, whose father and mother we know?" (Jn 6:42).

In the end, mocking the Eucharist while believing in the Incarnation is illogical and inconsistent. G.K. Chesterton eloquently lamented this lack of logic when he wrote this penetrating commentary:

> Heaven has descended into the world of matter; the supreme spiritual power is now operating by the machinery of matter, dealing miraculously with the bodies and souls of men. It blesses all the five senses . . . It works through water or oil or bread or wine. . . I cannot for the life of me understand why [a Protestant] does not see that the Incarnation is as much a part of that idea as the Mass. A Puritan may think it blasphemous that God should become a wafer. A Moslem thinks it blasphemous that God should become a workman of Galilee. . . . If it be profane that the miraculous should descend to the plan of matter, then certainly Catholicism is profane; and Protestantism is profane; and Christianity is profane. Of all human creeds and concepts, in that sense, Christianity is the most utterly profane. But why a man should accept a Creator who was a carpenter, and then worry about holy water . . . why he should accept the first and most stupendous part of the story of Heaven on Earth, and then furiously deny a few small but obvious deductions from it – that is a thing I do not understand." ("The Protestant Superstitions," *Collected Works*, vol. III [San Francisco: Ignatius Press, 1990] 258-259).

Historically, the sort of attacks on the Eucharist leveled by men such as McCarthy are drawn from several sources, including Docetism (second century), the Reformation (the 1500s), and Enlightenment-era rationalism (late 1700s). While differing in many ways, each of these movements gave birth to a symbolic understanding of the Eucharist. The Docetists were second-century Gnostics who believed that the Son only *seemed* to be human (*dokeo* is the Greek word for "seem"), but was actually a spirit. They believed that the spiritual realm alone is real and good, while the physical realm is illusory and temporary, possessing little or no value. Ignatius, the bishop of Antioch who was martyred around A.D. 110, condemned the Docetists for their refusal to accept the Real Presence, a stance based on their denial of Jesus' humanity: "They hold aloof from the Eucharist and from services of prayer, because they refuse to admit that the Eucharist is the flesh of our Savior Jesus Christ, which suffered for our sins . . ." (*Letter to the Smyrnaeans*, 6:2).

The correct interpretation of Jesus' statement in John 6:63 can be found by paying careful attention to what He says—and doesn't say. He says that *the* flesh profits nothing; He doesn't say that *His* flesh profits nothing. After all, if the Son's flesh is of no value, why did He become incarnate in the first place? Why did He undergo physical torment and suffering on the Cross? This understanding is obviously unacceptable to Christians. No, it makes far more sense to understand Jesus as saying that physical, material things have no value on their own—they need to be spiritually awakened, renewed, and transformed. The "fleshly" mind cannot comprehend the things of the Spirit.

This important truth is one that Paul emphasizes again and again in contrasting the flesh with the Spirit. "For the mind set on the flesh is death, but the mind set on the Spirit is life and peace," he writes to the Romans, "However, you are not in the flesh but in the Spirit, if indeed the Spirit of God dwells in you. But if anyone does not have the Spirit of Christ, he does not belong to Him" (Rom 8:6, 9). Writing to the Galatians, he states, "But I say, walk by the Spirit, and you will not carry out the desire of the flesh. For the flesh sets its desire against the Spirit, and the Spirit against the flesh; for these are in opposition to one another, so that you may not do the things that you please" (Gal 5:16-17).

Jesus' command to eat His flesh and drink His blood are to be taken literally and understood concretely, but with spiritual eyes and a spiritually enlightened mind. Without the Holy Spirit, we cannot be saved, nor can we understand the things of God. Jesus' words cannot be understood unless the Holy Spirit guides us into truth. Sadly, those who want to do away with His words by insisting that Catholics misuse and twist them end up missing out on Jesus' astonishing offer of true food and true drink.

Just a Meaty Metaphor?

"C'mon, Jeff," I've had Evangelical friends say to me, "Jesus is teaching by means of a metaphor that His listeners would understand. His Bread of Life discourse is completely metaphorical and is meant to teach us about our need for a personal relationship with Him." Or, as McCarthy writes, "The figurative interpretation [of the Eucharist] is consistent with Jesus' teaching on the nature of worship. He taught that 'God is spirit, and those who worship Him must worship in spirit and truth' (Jn 4:24). Since spiritual communion is the goal, Christ's bodily presence is unnecessary. Ordinary bread and wine can serve as adequate reminders for Christians as they gather to 'proclaim the Lord's death until He comes' (1 Cor 11:26). Then they will not need symbols, for they shall have Him!" (*The Gospel According to Rome*, 138).

Those are amazing words, and similar to ones that I used to preach to my congregation. But read them carefully and ask yourself: Is it true that we don't need Christ's bodily presence? That ordinary bread and wine are good enough? That they are "adequate"? Are we to believe that at the climactic point of His Bread of Life discourse, Jesus suddenly abandoned His strong, literal language and switched to metaphor? Such a poor teaching technique could only end in confusion. Should we suppose that God provided miraculous food in the Old Testament, but doesn't so after the Incarnation and Jesus' ministry, death, and resurrection? Is that really adequate or fitting?

No, it isn't, as Scripture shows. As we've seen, there's no denying that Jesus' references to Himself as the bread of life (vs. 35-51) are initially somewhat ambiguous and have a metaphorical flavor. But the key is in how Jesus Himself explains what He means by this title. He actually intensifies the matter by clearly saying that the bread is His flesh (v. 51). As Father Raymond Brown has noted, the Eucharistic theme of verses 51-58 "comes to the forefront and dominates the stage. Rather than the bread of life which must be received through faith, we now have the *living* bread which must be eaten (nay, "fed upon"—*trogo*), bread identified with the flesh of Jesus" ("The Eucharist and Baptism in John," *New Testament Essays* [New York: Paulist Press, 1965], 85).

Brown refers here to how the language used by Jesus changes in this latter section of John 6. The word for "eat" actually changes in the Greek from *phago*, a rather ordinary and mundane word, to *trogo*, which literally means to "gnaw or chew." Even *Vine's Expository Dictionary*, a venerable Protestant resource which adheres to the metaphorical interpretation of John 6 in its entirety, remarks: "In John 6, the change in the Lord's use from the verb 'phago' to the stronger verb 'trogo' is noticeable." In fact, the word *trogo* is never used symbolically in either the Bible or in ancient literature. In addition, if Jesus had said "Eat my flesh" in a metaphorical manner He would have been saying, "Revile me, destroy me" (see Ps 27:2; Micah 3:1-4; Is 9:18-20, Rv 17:6), making His words nonsensical. Talk about emphasizing a point! Jesus not only flatly states several times that His disciples must eat His flesh and drink His blood,

He uses language that is even more obvious and concrete than before.

Yet I used to believe, as do many Christians today, that eating the flesh and drinking the blood of Jesus is a metaphorical reference to believing in Him and having a personal relationship with Him as Lord and Savior. According to this interpretation, it has nothing to do with the Eucharist, or liturgy, or ritual. It's just a way of emphasizing the necessity of believing in Jesus.

Ironically, it is true that Jesus wants an intimate, personal relationship with Him—so personal, in fact, that He gives us His flesh and blood to receive into our bodies! But Jesus' listeners never indicate that they think He is using metaphorical language in verses 51 and following, and Jesus never offers that as an option. The people are clearly upset by what He is saying, but He doesn't change His words or explain them away. The tension is not the result of confusion over whether Jesus is speaking metaphorically or literally. No, the people are angry and upset with Jesus because He is demanding the kind of faith only God can demand—and many of them aren't willing to give it to Him. Their disbelief comes from a failure to recognize Jesus as God and to place their faith in Him. It is fine with them when He performs miracles that satisfy their stomachs, but they don't want any part of a miracle that challenges their hearts. They want Jesus to remain a good man and a nice prophet—not someone who requires an act of faith that causes discomfort and self-examination: "But there are some of you who do not believe" (v. 64).

In other places in the gospels where Jesus' teachings were difficult or puzzling, He would explain further, always making certain that His intended meaning was understood. In Matthew's Gospel there is the incident of the disciples forgetting to bring bread with them across the lake (Mt 16:5-12). Jesus tells them, "Watch out and beware of the leaven of the Pharisees and Sadducees." The disciples are confused and say, "It is because we took no bread" (v. 7). Jesus immediately and sharply corrects them:

> You men of little faith, why do you discuss among yourselves that you have no bread? ... How is it that you do not understand that I did not speak to you concerning bread? But beware of the leaven of the Pharisees and Sadducees." Then they understood that He did not say to beware of the leaven of bread, but of the teaching of the Pharisees and Sadducees (vs. 8, 11-12).

In John 4, at the conclusion of the well-known story of the Samaritan woman at the well, there is a similar situation. The disciples return after having gone to get food and ask Jesus to eat, "saying, 'Rabbi, eat.' But He said to them, 'I have food to eat that you do not know about.'" Again, the disciples were confused, saying to each other, "No one brought him anything to eat, did he?" And once again, Jesus explains the true meaning of His words: "My food is to do the will of him who sent me, and to accomplish his work" (Jn 4:31-34).

But there is no immediate correction of this sort at the end of John 6 for the simple reason that there was no misunderstanding. We know that this is the case because Jesus does not say, "But there are some of you who misunderstand," but instead declares, "But there are some of you who do not believe." (v. 64). And what have they not believed? "The words that I have spoken to you...." (v. 63). And those words were emphatic and repeated several times: "Eat my flesh and drink my blood" (vs. 53-57).

Despite all of this, many people try with all their might to escape the full meaning of Jesus' words. McCarthy writes that only the figurative interpretation of Jesus' words at the Last Supper and John 6—not the literal interpretation— "is reasonable. The disciples are not required to drink blood and eat human flesh. . . . And there is no need to invent complicated theories to explain away the obvious: The bread and wine remain bread and wine" (p. 136). He then lists a number of figurative statements made by Jesus, such as "I am the light of the world" (Jn 8:12), "I am the door" (Jn 10:9), and "I am the true vine" (Jn 15:1). McCarthy claims that Jesus' words at the Last Supper—"Take, eat; this is my body" and "This is my blood of the covenant" (Mt 26:26, 28)—and in John 6—"Eat My flesh, drink my blood"—are the same sort of statements: figurative, metaphorical, and symbolic.

At first glance, that seems to be a compelling argument—and the argument is made often. I once heard of a Protestant radio show host who said that Jesus' words were like a poet saying, "The road is a ribbon." It's a very pleasant, literary way of describing an ordinary thing in a poetic fashion. And, of course, if I stood on the road and said, "The road is a ribbon" no one would be bothered by it. It might even mean I am a poet of modest talent. But if I picked up a chunk of asphalt in my hand and said, "This *is* ribbon," people might start to wonder about my mental health.

Likewise, at the Last Supper, Jesus did not say, "I am a loaf of bread." He held the bread and broke it, saying, "Take, eat, *this is* my body." Similarly, in John 6 the people were not bothered when Jesus described Himself as the "bread of life" (v. 35, 48). And until verse 51 there is a certain ambiguity about the bread, even though there is none about Jesus' call to believe in Him. But no ambiguity or room for metaphor remains when He declares that "the bread also which I shall give for the life of the world is my flesh." If *that* is metaphor, then we are in trouble, since our salvation depends upon the death of Jesus' actual body of flesh and blood on the Cross!

Broken Bread, Whole Christ

Catholics are sometimes asked questions such as, "If you only eat half of a Communion wafer, did you only eat half of

Jesus?" or "If you don't drink from the cup, aren't you missing part of Jesus?" This confusion is understandable, although it is sometimes really meant to trip up the Catholic.

Such remarks reflect a misunderstanding of what the Catholic Church teaches about the Eucharist and the nature of the Eucharist. The *Catechism* states that "in the most blessed sacrament of the Eucharist 'the body and blood, together with the soul and divinity, of our Lord Jesus Christ and, therefore, *the whole Christ is truly, really, and substantially contained*.' 'This presence is called 'real'–by which is not intended to exclude the other types of presence as if they could not be 'real' too, but because it is presence in the fullest sense: that is to say, it is a *substantial* presence by which Christ, God and man, makes himself wholly and entirely present.'" (CCC 1374).

We do not believe we take just a piece of Christ's flesh, or a portion of Christ's blood, in the Eucharist. It is the entire Christ. That means the entire Incarnate Word, who is true God and true man, one Person with two natures mysteriously and perfectly brought together in the *hypostatic union* (i.e., two natures—divine and human—in one divine Person). Jesus, the Jewish carpenter who walked this earth in the early part of the first century, was completely human, yet also completely divine. So the Jesus of whom we partake in the Eucharist is completely human and completely divine. To separate the two is to attack a core tenet of the Christian Faith: the Incarnation.

After the consecration at Mass, Christ is fully present in the Sacred Host (which still appears to be bread) and in the Sacred Blood (which still has the appearances of wine). Again, as I pointed out earlier, Jesus is truly present, but in a unique mode that goes beyond our scientific methods of observation. It would be incorrect to think that only His Body is in the Sacred Host and only His Blood is in the cup.

He is totally present in both, since He cannot be divided. When a Host is broken, Christ is present in each part, wholly and completely. The same is true of each crumb and particle and drop. St. Thomas Aquinas beautifully expressed this mystery in his hymn *Lauda Sion*:

> When the sacramental sign is broken
> Have no doubts, rather remember that
> All is contained in the part as in the whole.
> For there is no dividing the reality,
> Only the sacramental sign is broken.
> The One signified is not affected in any way.

So it is the sign that is broken, not the Body of Christ. Can we fully understand this or begin to explain it? No. Just as we cannot fully understand or explain the mystery of the Trinity or the mystery of the Incarnation, we cannot fully comprehend or describe this mystery of the Eucharist. Like Peter, we simply say, "Lord, to whom shall we go? You have words of eternal life. And we have believed and have come to know that You are the Holy One of God" (Jn 6:68-69).

What About Those Other Passages?

I've written many pages discussing John 6, but it is not, of course, the only passage of Scripture that tells us about the Eucharist. The Eucharist is mentioned in the three synoptic Gospels in the Last Supper narratives (Mt 26:26-29; Mk 14:22-24; Lk 22:17-20) and is explicitly taught by Paul in 1 Corinthians 10 and 11.

There are several other references, including the Emmaus road narrative (Lk 24), the frequent mention in the Acts of the Apostles of the breaking of bread, a favorite Lucan theme (Acts 2:42), the description of the priesthood of Melchizedek in the Epistle to the Hebrews (Heb 5-7), and verses such as

Hebrews 13:10: "We have an altar, from which those who serve the tabernacle have no right to eat."

The Last Supper narratives fulfill the words of Jesus' found in John 6. On the night when He would be betrayed and arrested, Jesus and the disciples ate the Passover meal and celebrated the great feast of the Jews. The Lamb of God took the bread and wine, said a blessing, broke the bread, gave it to His disciples and said: "Take, eat; this is my body." He took the cup and gave thanks, then gave it to them and said, "Drink from it, all of you; for this is my blood of the covenant, which is poured out for many for forgiveness of sins" (Mt 26:26-29).

The connections and parallels are clear and striking. In John 6, Jesus declares at the time of the Passover that He is the bread of life sent from heaven. And He tells the people, "Truly, truly, I say to you, unless you eat the flesh of the Son of Man and drink His blood, you have no life in yourselves" (Jn 6:53). This is the life of the New Covenant, given in and by the broken body of the Passover Lamb, "who takes away the sin of the world!" (Jn 1:29). It is the perfect sacrifice of the perfect victim, who is also the perfect high priest:

> Because it is the memorial of Christ's Passover, the Eucharist is also a sacrifice. The sacrificial character of the Eucharist is manifested in the very words of institution: "This is my body which is given for you" and "This cup which is poured out for you is the New Covenant in my blood." In the Eucharist Christ gives us the very body which he gave up for us on the cross, the very blood which he "poured out for many for the forgiveness of sins" (CCC 1365).

One important connection involves the betrayal of Judas. In the synoptic Gospels, Judas' betrayal is described in the Last Supper accounts. John specifically mentions the betrayer at the conclusion of Jesus' Bread of Life discourse, immediately following Peter's statement of faith:

> Jesus answered them, "Did I myself not choose you, the twelve, and yet one of you is a devil?" Now he meant Judas the son of Simon Iscariot, for he, one of the twelve, was going to betray him (Jn 6:70-71).

Just like the Last Supper narratives recorded by Matthew, Mark, and Luke, John 6 begins with the Passover and ends with Judas' betrayal. They are bookends that alert the reader to the fact that this passage is about the Eucharistic Sacrifice and that it develops the sacramental theology of the early Church.

The story of the disciples on the Emmaus road powerfully portrays Jesus feeding His disciples and revealing Himself fully in the Eucharist. As Luke's description indicates, the disciples had lost their bearings and sense of direction in the overwhelming aftermath of Jesus' death: "And they stood still, looking sad" (Lk 24:17). They don't recognize the man who joins them. In response to His question, the men explain their confusion: Jesus was "a prophet mighty in deed and word" yet He had not fulfilled their hope for redemption (v. 21). In addition to this disappointment there was the added confusion of the empty tomb, although no conclusion seems to have been drawn from that fact. They are in shock and not able to think clearly. They are men in need of direction and purpose, hungry for answers to difficult questions.

Jesus chides them and takes them to the Scriptures, "beginning with Moses and with all the prophets" (v. 27), to show them the true nature of the Christ. Among the passages that Jesus probably showed them are: Deuteronomy 18:15 ("a prophet" like Moses), Psalm 2:7 ("Thou art my son") and Isaiah 53 (the Suffering Servant). The latter passage from the great Old Testament prophet would have been especially powerful and poignant:

> Surely our griefs he himself bore, and our sorrows he carried; yet we ourselves esteemed him stricken, smitten of God, and

> afflicted. But he was pierced through for our transgressions, he was crushed for our iniquities; the chastening for our well-being fell upon him, and by his scourging we are healed. All of us like sheep have gone astray, each of us has turned to his own way; But the Lord has caused the iniquity of us all To fall on him. He was oppressed and he was afflicted, Yet he did not open his mouth; Like a lamb that is led to slaughter, And like a sheep that is silent before its shearers, So he did not open his mouth (Is 53:4-7).

The disciples had to see that salvation and glory was to come, not through political or social upheaval, but through humiliation, suffering, and apparent defeat. The Lamb had to be slaughtered so that His life could be offered to all.

There had to be a re-learning, a new understanding of Scriptures so familiar, in order for the disciples to grasp all that had happened, to see that it had gone according to plan, and that it offered hope—not despair. This education came from the very One who sent the prophets and gave them words—who better to illuminate their true meaning? The distinct pattern of questioning, dialogue, and exposition of Scripture, leading up to the celebration of a sacrament, is a Lucan formula that is found again in Acts 8 with the story of the Ethiopian eunuch.

While a few scholars have downplayed or denied the spiritual significance of the breaking of bread with the disciples in Emmaus (Lk 24:30), most agree that it is indeed Eucharistic. In fact, this event and its fuller meaning cannot be really appreciated unless its Eucharistic character is admitted. A failure to comprehend the sacramental order and the incarnational dimensions of Jesus' life, death, and resurrection will leave a reader in puzzlement over this passage. But when read with a knowledge of the Eucharist's centrality in the Church, the passage begins to yield clues and insights into the mystery of Jesus and the recognition of

Him, finally, by the disciples "in the breaking of the bread" (v. 35).

The Eucharist is at the core of all true knowledge of the Incarnate One and of His mission, fulfilled through His Church. This is powerfully demonstrated by the Risen Lord's act of taking the bread, blessing it, breaking it, and giving it to them (v. 30)—the same actions that occurred at the Last Supper. At that moment, "their eyes were opened and they recognized Him; and He vanished from their sight" (v. 31). When they return to Jerusalem and report these wondrous events to the eleven apostles, they relate what they experienced on the road "and how He was recognized by them in the breaking of the bread" (v. 35).

It was a supernatural act that opened their eyes, an act that was intimately connected with the "breaking of bread." Yet the breaking of bread was not only an act, but also a reality—the reality of the Christ fully revealing Himself. It was the culmination of His revelation from Scripture, completely realized in the most humble of acts, breaking bread and feeding His followers. It is no coincidence that the liturgy of the Church recognizes Jesus in the Liturgy of the Word and consumes Him in the Liturgy of the Eucharist. As in Emmaus, both the Scriptures and the Eucharist bear witness to Him and instruct His Church about His true identity and what His Church is called to be and to do on earth.

In his first letter to the Christians in Corinth, Paul exhorts them to live pure lives and to have nothing to do with pagan religions and sacrifices. "Is not the cup of blessing which we bless a sharing in the blood of Christ?" he asks, "Is not the bread which we break a sharing in the body of Christ?" (1 Cor 10:16). His concern is for both purity and unity: "Since there is one bread, we who are many are one body; for we all partake of the one bread" (1 Cor 10:17).

That bread is the body of Jesus, as Paul explains in the next chapter, where he describes the events of the Last Supper and Jesus' words.

> For I received from the Lord that which I also delivered to you, that the Lord Jesus in the night in which He was betrayed took bread; and when He had given thanks, He broke it, and said, "This is My body, which is for you; do this in remembrance of me." In the same way He took the cup also, after supper, saying, "This cup is the new covenant in my blood; do this, as often as you drink it, in remembrance of Me" (1 Cor 11:23-25).

These are familiar words, but Paul adds a strong warning that clearly expresses the fact that the Eucharist is not a symbol: "Therefore whoever eats the bread or drinks the cup of the Lord in an unworthy manner, shall be guilty of the body and the blood of the Lord" (1 Cor 11:27). Of this verse, St. John Chrysostom writes, "It is like those who pierced Jesus on the cross. They did not do it in order to drink His blood but in order to shed it. The person who comes to the supper unworthily does much the same and gains nothing by it." We must carefully examine ourselves, Paul writes, before receiving the body and blood of Christ.

Isn't it interesting that the author of Hebrews also writes "We have an altar, from which those who serve the tabernacle have no right to eat" (Heb 13:10)? Every time we go to Mass it is an altar call! And when we go forward to the altar, with the greatest of love and reverence, it is to partake of what John describes in the book of Revelation as the "hidden manna" (Rv 2:17), the sacramental food, the mystery of faith. Jesus is hidden, but He does not hide—He gives Himself and reveals Himself completely.

Chapter 10

The Fathers Know Best

The great patristics scholar J. N. D. Kelly, in his classic work *Early Christian Doctrines*, wrote that in the early Church "Eucharistic teaching, it should be understood at the outset, was in general unquestioningly realist, i.e., the consecrated bread and wine were taken to be, and were treated and designated as, the Savior's body and blood" (p. 440).

The witness of the early Church is in overwhelming agreement: The Eucharist is Christ's Body and Blood, and John 6 is most definitely about the Eucharist. Contrary opinions were very late in developing, and date back to the twelfth or thirteenth centuries, at the earliest. Even Martin Luther believed the Eucharist was much more than a metaphor, teaching that Jesus was really present along with, or consubstantial with, the bread and wine. John Calvin believed there was a powerful spiritual presence in the Eucharist, but denied that any transformation took place. It was Ulrich Zwingli, the leader of the most radical Protestants, who really solidified the belief that the Eucharist—along with all of the sacraments—was only a symbol and nothing more. These beliefs were articulated and developed in the 1520s and 1530s, a full 1,500 years after Jesus' Resurrection and Ascension!

When, as a Protestant, I began reading the early Church Fathers, it was because I realized that these men followed directly in the footsteps of the Apostles and their disciples, and so their thoughts and insights deserved seriously consideration. I suspended judgment about what I thought they should have written about and attempted to read them within the context of their own era. The majority of them died for the Christian faith, all of them believed that the Eucharist is the true Body and Blood of Christ, and most of them refer to the episcopal nature of Church authority, including the central place of the See of Rome.

Some Fundamentalists teach that the early Church apostatized very early from the true faith, perhaps within a decade or two of Jesus' Ascension. They insist that the Bible alone should be our guide as Christians, and that the writings of the Church Fathers should be ignored, or at least do not deserve much time and attention. Nevertheless, if it weren't for those early Church bishops and theologians, we wouldn't even have a Bible, or know which books belong in it.

This brings us once again to the key question: Where does the authority reside to determine what is orthodox teaching or false teaching? An examination of the Church councils, including the Jerusalem Council, is instructive in this regard. When controversies and disagreements arose in the early Church, both sides inevitably pointed to the Old Testament and assorted Church writings to validate their beliefs. This was true of the Marcionites, the Arians, the Sabellians and all the rest. Irenaeus, a theologian who lived in the second century, comments on this phenomenon in his classic work *Against Heresies*. And he declares quite strikingly that an appeal to Scripture alone was not the solution:

> Yet when we appeal again to that tradition which is derived from the Apostles, and which is safeguarded in the churches through the succession of presbyters, they then are adversaries of tradition, claiming to be wiser not only than the presbyters but even than the Apostles, and to have discovered the truth

> undefiled...Thus it comes about that they now agree neither with the Scriptures nor with tradition...Those who wish to discern the truth may observe the apostolic tradition made manifest in every church throughout the world. We can enumerate those who were appointed bishops in the churches by the Apostles, and their successors down to our own day...[we point] to the apostolic tradition and the faith that is preached to men, which has come down to us through the succession of bishops; the tradition and creed of the greatest, the most ancient church, the church known to all men, which was founded and set up at Rome by the two most glorious Apostles, Peter and Paul. For with this church, because of its position of leadership and authority, must needs agree every church, that is, the faithful everywhere; for in her the apostolic tradition has always been preserved by the faithful from all parts" (*Adversus Haereses*, III)

The same Fundamentalists who ignore the writings of the Church Fathers will sometimes claim that the Mass was not instituted by Jesus, but was a false practice instituted in A.D. 394, or some date following the reign of the Emperor Constantine in the early 300s. However, as we've seen, while some of the externals of the Mass—certain prayers, music, and ceremonies—have changed, the central actions and meaning have always been the same. As we've seen, the Mass was instituted by Christ at the Last Supper when He took the bread and said, "Take, eat; this is My body" (Mt 26:26) and when He took the cup and said, "Drink from it, all of you; for this is My blood of the covenant, which is poured out for many for forgiveness of sins" (Mt 26:28). And Paul writes, the Lord commanded that this be done "in remembrance of Me . . .For as often as you eat this bread and drink the cup, you proclaim the Lord's death until He comes" (1 Cor 11:24-26).

If the true teaching had been that the Eucharist was merely symbolic, wouldn't the historical evidence give some indication of this? Yet all the evidence upholds Catholic teaching: The bread and wine truly and sacramentally become the body and blood of Christ. As we saw earlier, Ignatius of Antioch, a disciple of the Apostle John, was clear about this point:

> Take note of those who hold heterodox opinions on the grace of Jesus Christ which has come to us, and see how contrary their opinions are to the mind of God. . . . They [he refers to the Docetists, who denied God became man] abstain from the Eucharist and from prayer because they do not confess that the Eucharist is the flesh of our Savior Jesus Christ, flesh which suffered for our sins and which the Father, in his goodness, raised up again. They who deny the gift of God are perishing in their disputes. (*Letter to the Smyrnaeans*, 6:2-7:1, [A.D. 110]).

Justin Martyr, the second-century Christian apologist who was a philosopher and a convert from paganism, wrote:

> And this food is called among us Eucharist, of which no one is allowed to partake but the man who believes that the things which we teach are true, and who has been washed with the washing that is for the remission of sins, and unto regeneration, and who is so living as Christ has enjoined. For not as common bread and common drink do we receive these; but in like manner as Jesus Christ our Savior, having been made flesh by the Word of God, had both flesh and blood for our salvation, so likewise have we been taught that the food which is blessed by the prayer of His word, and from which our blood and flesh by transmutation are nourished, is the flesh and blood of that Jesus who was made flesh. (*First Apology*, 66, [A.D. 151]).

This view of the Eucharist, consistently taught for 2,000 years, is the basis for understanding the Mass as a sacrifice. The Catholic Church has always taught that there is only one sacrifice, and that is the sacrifice of Christ on the Cross. There is no Catholic doctrine to the contrary. But the anti-Catholic makes the mistake, all too often, of not finding out what the Church really teaches.

From the very beginning, the Church understood that celebrating the Eucharist in memory of the Lord Jesus is not a mere symbol or metaphor, but an actual re-presentation of the once-for-all and unique suffering, death, and resurrection of Christ, the Paschal Mystery. The fancy word for this re-presentation is *anamnesis*, a Greek word meaning "recalling to mind." But this goes far beyond a mental recollection or a subjective reaction to past events. When Jews celebrated the Passover, they did not celebrate Passover Number 1,248 or 2,184. They celebrated only one Passover, the one that had taken place in Egypt centuries and centuries ago. There is a single Passover, and it was present to them as truly as it was to those being led out of Egypt by Moses. That one-time historical event has meaning and power that transcends history; by the power of God they relived and experienced that salvific event.

The same truth applies to the sacrifice of Jesus the Christ on the Cross. Historically, it occurred 2,000 years ago. But it was not an ordinary historical event, for it involved the suffering and death of the God-man, whose influence and power extends far beyond space and time. At Mass, we come into contact with the ongoing power and reality of what happened that day at Golgotha. The crucified and risen Lord is no longer on the Cross, but He comes to us with all of the blessings and graces that He earned for our sake on the Cross, and then offers Himself—grace personified—in the Eucharist. At Mass, time stands still and we are drawn into the heavenly liturgical celebration. Immediately after seeing the throne room of God, filled with endless praise and chants of "Holy, holy, holy, is the Lord God, the Almighty, who was and who is and who is to come" (Rv 4:8), John sees Someone else: "And I saw between the throne (with the four living creatures) and the elders a Lamb standing, as if slain, having seven horns and seven eyes, which are the seven Spirits of

God, sent out into all the earth" (Rv 5:6). The Lamb has ascended into heaven, and now by the power of Holy Spirit through the Mass He continues to give Himself to us and to build up His Body of saints.

Fundamentalists will have none of this, of course. The irony is that most anti-Catholic Fundamentalists actually believe in something somewhat similar: being "washed by the blood of Christ." This refers to their belief that upon asking Jesus to be their "personal Lord and Savior," they are covered by His blood, a reference to Revelation 7:14 and the saints who "have washed their robes and made them white in the blood of the Lamb." But if Christ's work on the Cross is finished, how can someone be "washed in the blood of the Lamb"? Does it not imply that Christ is still bleeding, that is, still being sacrificed? Of course not. It refers to the fact that the salvific work of the Crucifixion—which took place in time and space—is just as powerful and efficacious now as it was then. But how is that so? How is the efficacy of an event that took place in time and space 2,000 years ago being applied to someone living today? By virtue of the fact that Jesus was both human and divine, therefore the effects of His sacrifice are eternal and not bound by space and time. Because of this great mystery, the Mass truly is a participation in the same, once-for-all sacrifice of Christ. In the Mass, Christ gives Himself to His Body on earth; we in turn offer ourselves to God the Father through the Person of Christ, in the power of the Holy Spirit.

The testimony of the early Church provides further evidence of this understanding of the Mass. Again, this teaching was not challenged until well into the second millennium. In the *Didache*, the earliest known non-canonical Christian writing (c. A.D. 70-90), we read:

> Assemble on the Lord's Day, and break bread and offer the Eucharist; but first make confession of your faults, so that

> your sacrifice may be a pure one. Anyone who has a difference with his fellow is not to take part with you until they have been reconciled, so as to avoid any profanation of your sacrifice [see Mt 5:23-24]. For this is the offering of which the Lord has said, "Everywhere and always bring me a sacrifice that is undefiled, for I am a great king, says the Lord, and my name is the wonder of nations" [Mal 1:11, 14] (*Didache* 14).

Justin Martyr makes reference to a passage quoted quite often by many of the early Church Fathers, the first chapter of Malachi:

> God speaks by the mouth of Malachi, one of the twelve [minor prophets], as I said before, about the sacrifices at that time presented by you [Jews]: "I have no pleasure in you, says the Lord, and I will not accept your sacrifices at your hands; for from the rising of the sun to the going down of the same, my name has been glorified among the Gentiles, and in every place incense is offered to my name, and a pure offering, for my name is great among the Gentiles . . ." [Mal. 1:10-11]. He then speaks of those Gentiles, namely us [Christians] who in every place offer sacrifices to him, that is, the bread of the Eucharist and also the cup of the Eucharist. (*Dialogue with Trypho the Jew* 41 [A.D. 155]).

To Whom Shall We Go?

Many other quotes are available, all giving unanimous testimony to the Church's consistent and clear teaching that the Mass is a sacrifice: the Body and Blood of Jesus truly made present under the appearances of bread and wine. This sacramental transubstantiation of bread and wine into the flesh and blood of the Passover Lamb is a divine act accomplished by Jesus Christ Himself, acting through His ordained minister, the priest.

Jesus said, "No one can come to me unless it has been granted them by the Father." As a result of this, many of His disciples withdrew and were not walking with Him anymore.

Many of them left. They couldn't handle the truth. Jesus doesn't stop them. Instead, He looks at His apostles and asks them, "You do not want to go away also, do you?" Simon Peter answered him, "Lord, to whom shall we go? You have the words of eternal life." We should ask ourselves: To whom shall we go? If we do not receive this Eucharist, where are we going to go? What will you and I exchange for the very Body and Blood of Jesus Christ? A better song? One that makes you feel happy? A home group full of fellowship where we can read the Bible together? An exciting prayer meeting? A rousing sermon? What *did* we exchange the Eucharist for, and what are you getting out of that today? What are you being fed?

Two thousand years ago at the synagogue in Capernaum, many of Jesus' disciples walked out on Him. "This is a difficult statement," they said, "Who can listen to it?" It is still a difficult issue for many today. Jesus' words demand faith and humility and love. They demand that we give ourselves to the One who gave Himself for us—and still does, every day. We bring Him our bread; we bring Him the wine. We bring Him our sufferings, pain, and struggles. We bring Him our weakness and failings. We bring all of these things and, by the power of the Incarnate Word, the bread is changed into the Body and Blood of Christ. He then gives us His very Flesh to eat and His very Blood to drink, so that by the power of the Holy Spirit we can be united with Christ in Holy Communion.

That's the Good Shepherd, the perfect Shepherd who loves us. He gives His life in order to save those who are lost. We have this astonishing exchange. But do we *live* as though we believe this? Do we *live* as people who are receiving this perfect gift? Recently, a man came up to me and said, "Jeff, if I believed what you believe about the Eucharist, I would be at Mass every single time those doors opened. I don't think you believe in the real presence of Christ in the Eucharist. If that is the Body and Blood of Christ, you would crave it. You would desire it with everything in your being." Those are challenging words, and I appreciate them. We need the challenge to remind us of who we are and Who He is.

We, as Catholics, are fed on a diet of the Word of God and we are fed by Jesus' Body and Blood. This all takes place in the Mass, a most beautiful and sacred reality. I appeal to those who have left the Catholic Church: come back home. The banquet table is still set. The Lamb stands, waiting. The Shepherd calls, waiting. But hurry, for the time is near (Rv 1:3).

Chapter 11

The *Real* Meal Deal

Do you remember the "lady with the dietary deficiency" at the beginning of this book? "Jeff," she said to me, "I heard that you went back to the Catholic Church. That's good for you. I was in the Church for thirty years, but I had to leave because *I wasn't being fed*."

Here's the rest of the conversation. I got to talking with her and eventually asked, "Do you believe in the power of the Word? Do you believe what the prophets said, that the Word shall go forth and not return void, but it shall accomplish that which I desire"?

"Yes," she said, "of course."

"Do you believe that the Word of God is active and sharp and can penetrate to the bone and the marrow and the Spirit and soul?"

"Yes!"

"Do you believe that it will have an impact on your heart?"

"Yes!"

"How long did you attend the Catholic Church?"

"Thirty years, every week..."

I paused. "Do you realize that in the Catholic Church you get a cycle of three readings—the Old Testament, an Epistle, and a Gospel— and that, over a three-year period, you will hear almost the entire New Testament and all of the critical points of the Old Testament?"

She didn't say anything, but I could tell this was news to her.

"So, for thirty years, you heard almost the entire Bible not once, or three times, but *ten times*! And you spent thirty years receiving the very Body and Blood of Jesus Christ into your body! But, after thirty years of listening to the Word and taking the Word into your body, what's the first thing you did? You back-handed the mother who fed you for thirty years."

She appeared stunned at the combination of my passion and the content of my reply. Soon afterward she thanked me for the conversation and hurried off.

Listen to the Voice of the Shepherd

Unfortunately, stories like hers are fairly common, which is the main reason I first gave a talk entitled "I'm Not Being Fed! The #1 Catholic Eating Disorder" and decided to write a book on the same topic. People regularly come up to me or call me and tell me that when they were Catholics they didn't know anything, they weren't taught anything, they weren't being fed, they were wasting away spiritually, and they never read the Bible. And yet, in almost every case these same people, within a month of leaving the Church, become experts on the Catholic Church, the history of Catholicism, and Catholic theology and practice. While sitting in the parish pew they didn't know the difference between the hypostatic union and a hydraulic brake, but now they feel confident lecturing Catholics on the endless errors of Catholic theology! Perhaps you've encountered this situation with a friend or a family member.

I have a theory. It is this: When Catholics leave the Church and join the local New Hope Faith Center or start attending Pastor Bob's home group they start to have hunger pangs. At first, these pangs are very small. Those former Catholics feel them, perhaps unconsciously, and try to ignore or get rid of them. They study, go to church, attend Bible studies, and evangelize. They also confront Catholics and tell them why they need to leave the Church and save their souls from likely damnation. The hunger pangs increase. They are beginning to starve, but they aren't sure why. Though they don't yet know it, they are missing the Eucharist. I have met so many Catholics who, like me, walked away from the Church and the Mass for many years, sometimes decades. They all say the same thing: "I missed the Eucharist! I missed receiving the Lord!" They had left the Church for one reason or another and eventually realized that they weren't being fully fed apart from Holy Communion.

In many of these cases, God has been working on those peoples' hearts and minds for many years, until they finally said, "Yes, Lord! I want to know you more!" But instead of recognizing Him in the breaking of the bread, as did the disciples on the Emmaus Road, they think they have finally "discovered" Him at the local Assemblies of God, or at a Wednesday morning Baptist Bible study, or at the corner church where they have a drum set and a good guitar player. Yes, we naturally long for "change" and for what seems to be a more exciting and entertaining style of worship or sermon. But we Catholics have the Eucharist, the Body and Blood of our Lord Jesus Christ. We have the Bread of Life, the Hidden Manna, and "the one bread that provides the medicine of immortality, the antidote for death, and the food that makes us live for ever in Jesus Christ" (Ignatius of Antioch, *Letter to the Ephesians*, quoted in CCC 1405). By God's grace, we are no longer in the desert, but on the hillside. Jesus is before us and His apostles bring Him to us. "Eat my flesh and drink my blood."

Many say that they weren't being fed. In all honesty, however, many of them would have to admit they weren't being entertained, or made to feel special, or welcomed warmly enough after Mass. They grumble and they complain. I know what I'm talking about. I know the pressure of having to bring in a better singing group next month than the one that visited last month. I know what would happen if my preaching ever weakened or if my smile wasn't natural enough: People would leave and go find a better preacher, a more exciting worship experience, more comfortable pews, or more programs for the kids. I *know* this for a fact.

So, we'll say, "The church down the street has such vibrant worship. It has such incredible Bible studies. The pastor is on fire." All those things are good and fine, and I'm not making light of them. After all, we need priests who are on fire. We need priests who rejoice in the faith and are dynamic witnesses to the Gospel. There's no doubt that the Church, especially here in the United States, is often weak and fraught with problems. But Catholics need to take responsibility for themselves, to educate themselves, to seek truth, and to not be enticed by appeals to emotions. They need to work at learning what the Church teaches. As I said before, God's grace is free, but it isn't cheap. Prepare to have fellow Catholics annoy and upset you, priests who might offend you, and bishops who may frustrate you. But realize that the Good Shepherd laid down His life for all of us because "all have sinned and fall short of the glory of God" (Rom 3:23). Remember, we are sheep: often weak, ignorant, and nearsighted. We need to be fed, otherwise we'd starve out in the wilderness of this world.

At the close of the last chapter I quoted that wonderful verse from the last book of the Bible: "Behold I stand at the door and knock. If anyone hears my voice and opens the door, I will come into him and will dine with him, and he with me." I think it is a striking metaphor: "I stand at the door and knock." In John's Gospel, Jesus declares, "My sheep hear my voice. I am the Good Shepherd and the sheep hear my voice…" Where is that voice to be found? In Rome! The Holy Father! The Magisterium! The Tradition and Scripture! The Shepherd speaks to us in all of these interdependent ways, providing us with the full word of God, the deposit of faith: "If anyone hears my voice and opens the door, I will come into him and dine with him and him with me."

Enter the Mystery of the Eucharist

We have a meal that goes beyond anything we could ever conceive of by our human imagination. I will not trade in the Body and Blood of Christ. It is The Reason why I came back to the Church. I will never forget sitting in the back of the local parish, my head hung low, quietly weeping because I recognized that Jesus was in front of me, but I had to wait to receive Him. When I first gave the talk that is the basis for this book, I broke down in the middle of it and wept at the podium. Those were tears of thanksgiving that the Good Shepherd had sought me out while I was wandering in the desert. They were tears of humility as I considered the Body that was broken and the Blood that was shed on my behalf. There is no Bible study in the world that is good enough or stimulating enough or nutritious enough to substitute for the very Body and Blood of Jesus Christ. There's no song moving enough to replace the Body and Blood of Jesus Christ.

Catholics have a fullness to be enjoyed, a fullness to share with the entire world. We need to get up off our seats, and begin to live this God-given life, and begin to evangelize, and go out into the desert and proclaim the Good News. We need to live in such a way that people will say, "I see that they love each other, they care for each other, and I want what they have. Those people are fulfilled at the Table of the

Lord. I want to have what they receive. I want to eat what they are eating."

If you have left the Catholic Church, I want to invite you back to the banquet table. Visit with a priest about your journey home. It is always good to go to confession and cleanse your heart before receiving the wonderful sacrament of the Eucharist.

Sure, there are problems in the Church, but what family doesn't have problems? Noah had problems, Moses had problems, David had problems, and so did Saul. But this is why we need as much of Christ as we can get. There simply is no greater source of grace in the world than the Eucharist. Humble yourself before the King of Kings and allow Him to satisfy your soul. He died to feed you.

At the conclusion of *Ecclesia de Eucharistia*, John Paul II writes these powerful, challenging words:

> The mystery of the Eucharist – sacrifice, presence, banquet – does not allow for reduction or exploitation; it must be experienced and lived in its integrity, both in its celebration and in the intimate converse with Jesus which takes place after receiving communion or in a prayerful moment of Eucharistic adoration apart from Mass. These are times when the Church is firmly built up and it becomes clear what she truly is: one, holy, catholic and apostolic; the people, temple and family of God; the body and bride of Christ, enlivened by the Holy Spirit; the universal sacrament of salvation and a hierarchically structured communion. . . In the humble signs of bread and wine, changed into his body and blood, Christ walks beside us as our strength and our food for the journey, and he enables us to become, for everyone, witnesses of hope. If, in the presence of this mystery, reason experiences its limits, the heart, enlightened by the grace of the Holy Spirit, clearly sees the response that is demanded, and bows low in adoration and unbounded love. (par. 61)

Food for the journey has been given to us. We have been fed. We are being fed. "Lord, to whom shall we go? You have words of eternal life. And we have believed and have come to know that you are the Holy One of God." Amen.

Acknowledgments

Many thanks to Carl Olson, for his creative contributions to the manuscript; Fr. John Klockman, for his theological review and many helpful suggestions; Matthew Pinto and his team at Ascension Press for bringing this book to print; Elena Perri and Michael J. Miller for their editorial assistance; and to Kinsey Caruth for his cover design.

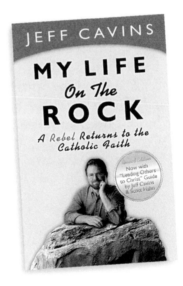